Published & distributed by:
Indiana Humanities

in association with:
IBJ Book Publishing
41 E. Washington St., Suite 200
Indianapolis, IN 46204
www.ibjbp.com

Indiana Humanities
1500 North Delaware Street
Indianapolis, IN 46202
317.638.1500

ISBN 978-1-934922-75-0
First Edition

Library of Congress Control Number: 2012941971

Printed in the United States of America

IndianaHumanities.org
IndianaHarvest.com

FOOD *for* THOUGHT

an INDIANA HARVEST

DAVID HOPPE | PHOTOGRAPHY BY KRISTIN HESS

FOREWORD

There is a food renaissance taking place in Indiana. It's happening in urban gardens and on large-scale farms; in laboratories and in food pantries; in upscale restaurants and in food trucks.

And it's happening because of people like you. Your hunger to support Indiana-grown products and creative, locally owned restaurants has helped contribute to this regeneration.

In early 2010, Indiana Humanities set out to better understand that hunger through Food for Thought, a two-year program designed to help Hoosiers think, read, and talk about food. We asked Hoosiers to share their stories, recipes, and traditions. We encouraged them to try new flavors, venture into new territories, and learn about other cultures. And we asked

them to sit down, break bread, and chat— or, as we so often said, to "chew on this."

The people of Indiana didn't disappoint us.

As we crisscrossed the state with a traveling exhibition and a variety of public programs designed to entice people to talk about food, we met Hoosiers eager to dish out stories about what food means to them. As we chatted at county fairs, city celebrations, farmers markets, and local eateries, we noted the pride they take in family favorites and community traditions. As we met in diners, kitchens, coffee shops, and community centers, we heard delight in their voices as they remembered special treats or familiar flavors. As we shared breakfasts, lunches, dinners, and desserts—there was *always* dessert—we savored the tales they told

about a revered restaurant, a relative's beloved recipe, a treasured dinnertime memory, or a bountiful harvest.

Through those stories, memories, and recipes, we saw the Hoosier spirit reflected again and again. We recognized the artisanal pride and connection to home that comes from preserving and perfecting traditional Indiana foods. We glimpsed the pioneering Hoosier spirit in growers, restaurateurs, and others who charge head-on into the challenges of making a living through food. We experienced the creative, entrepreneurial passion that drives people to take risks and introduce food-based innovations. We witnessed the sense of community that embraces so many independent and family-run operations. And we observed

It's our hope that the spirit of our two-year Food for Thought adventure will continue to thrive throughout Indiana, and that this book will help keep it alive.

real efforts to solve the food-based challenges across the street and around the globe.

In other words, we found the very things we set out looking for: We found Indiana and its people, as expressed through food. Time and time again, we also heard that this—today—is a great moment in Indiana food.

With this one-of-a-kind book that aims to capture that renaissance, we share a sampling of the people we met and a taste of the stories we heard through Food for Thought. Selected as a representative slice of the food culture we encountered in Indiana, *Food for Thought: An Indiana Harvest,* was cooked up by author David Hoppe and photographer/designer Kristin Hess after they spent months pursuing stories from every corner of the state.

Drawn from rural farm fields to urban dining rooms, from high-tech labs to low-tech eateries, and from global corporate enterprises to tiny mom-and-pop shops, the loving portraits on these pages are like wonderful meals. They offer the familiar and the surprising, a taste of something beloved and a hint of something unknown, and a sense of fulfillment along with a hunger for more. They amuse, intrigue, and satisfy. And, most important perhaps, they offer you an excuse to sit down with someone to talk about common experiences and points of difference.

It's our hope that the spirit of our two-year Food for Thought adventure will continue to thrive throughout Indiana and that this book will help keep the conversation alive. So, please: Eat it up. Savor it. Digest it. And share a portion with someone you love or someone you just met, spicing things up with a few stories of your own.

In that process, you will celebrate and perpetuate Indiana's rich food-based culture, and you will become a part of the wonderful, bountiful collection of stories we call *Food for Thought: An Indiana Harvest.*

Keira Amstutz
President and CEO, Indiana Humanities

INTRODUCTION

Food, like landscape, is easily taken for granted. We eat it, we travel through it and, too often, we forget about it.

People who live in Indiana know something about this.

Indiana, we are frequently reminded (usually by ourselves), is a state without mountains or ocean views. Our landscape lacks the visual crescendos movies and advertising have taught us to associate with lives lived big.

As for food, well, there's the breaded pork tenderloin.

We are justly proud of a certain modesty in our temperament, but modesty neither explains nor justifies overlooking the natural wonders afforded by the state's woodlands and prairies, marshes and dunes. There is plenty here to reward anyone who is willing to pay attention.

Happily, the only attention required of those who eat—which is all of us—is that we take a bite. And when it comes to Indiana's contemporary food scene, what's happening doesn't merely challenge stereotypes; it purees them.

For the better part of a year, photographer (and Indiana Humanities staff member) Kristin Hess and I traveled Indiana, meeting farmers and chefs, educators and activists. We recorded their stories and captured their images. Through this process, we created what amounts to a chorus of voices and a composite portrait comprised of individuals who are contributing to this burgeoning scene.

Unanimity is almost impossible to come by in a society as complex as ours. But, when it comes to what's happening today with Indiana food, that is what we found. No matter who we talked to, from old-timers to newcomers, everyone agreed this was the most dynamic time they could remember or had ever seen.

This phenomenon is not unique to Indiana. Wherever you go, it seems people are more aware of what they eat, what's in it, and how it is prepared. This is an age of celebrity chefs, the Food Network, and, it must also be said, massive food recalls due to occasionally tainted products.

But even within this larger context, what's happening in Indiana stands out. This has partly to do with our history. Geologically, the state's landscape was

No matter who we talked to, from old-timers to newcomers, everyone agreed this was the most dynamic time they could remember, or had ever seen.

formed by glacial movements, endowing the place with a particularly rich mix of soils. Even before its settlement, the land that came to be known as Indiana was cultivated by the Indians.

European settlers who migrated to Indiana put down roots of their own, establishing a tradition of family farming that continues to this day. In modern America, where families are extended, blended, and, too often, atomized, it is striking to see how often stories of family continuity, albeit skipping a generation here and there, are found at the heart of Hoosier agriculture.

There is also a story here about the remarkable number of creative individuals for whom Indiana's agricultural history and traditions have provided a ready source of inspiration for the development of new ventures, including urban and organic farming, sustainable livestock ranching, retail businesses and restaurants.

At times, it almost seems as if the entrepreneurial impulse evident in Indiana's food renaissance is a reflexive response to the state's manufacturing decline. In any event, it adds a homegrown, handcrafted dimension to the state's economic portfolio. With some of the top chefs in the country seeking products from some of our local producers, the words "Made in Indiana" signal a newfound energy.

What makes this even more remarkable is the fact that at the same time Indiana is experiencing this bottom-up groundswell, it is also home to an array of corporate brands that infuse Hoosier agriculture with a truly global reach.

This juxtaposition of the global and local in Indiana's food scene is perhaps the greatest contributor to its dynamism. It accounts for a creative tension that has the largest purveyors exploring new approaches to sustainability and upstart producers collaborating on new and more efficient ways to expand their markets.

Harvest is definitely here for Indiana food. This book is just one of the signs. Meet the people in these pages; you'll have a hard time taking what you eat for granted ever again.

David Hoppe
Indianapolis, March 2012

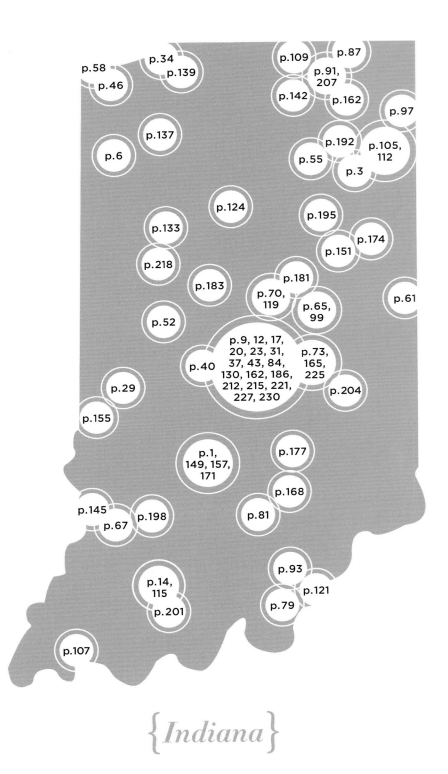

p.58

p.34

p.139

p.109   p.87

p.46

p.91,
207

p.142   p.162

p.137

p.97

p.6

p.192   p.105,
112

p.55

p.3

p.124

p.195

p.133

p.174

p.218

p.151

p.183

p.181

p.70,
119

p.65,
99

p.52

p.9, 12, 17,
20, 23, 31,
37, 43, 84,
130, 162, 186,
212, 215, 221,
227, 230

p.73,
165,
225

p.40

p.29

p.204

p.155

p.1,
149, 157,
171

p.177

p.168

p.145

p.81

p.67   p.198

p.93

p.14,
115

p.121

p.79

p.201

p.107

{*Indiana*}

STORIES

PLACE

Marcia Veldman — 1
Bloomington Community Farmers' Market

Pete and Alice Eshelman — 3
Joseph Decuis

Gary Corbett — 6
Fair Oaks Farms

Laura and Tyler Henderson — 9
Growing Places Indy

Kay Grimm and Sue Spicer — 12
Fruit Loop Acres

Alan Hanselman — 14
Schnitzelbank Restaurant

Becky Hostetter — 17
Duos

Jane and Fritz Kunz — 20
Traders Point Creamery

Cindy Hoye — 23
Indiana State Fair

RISK

Mike Roe — 29
Bridgeton Mill

Joe Vuskovich — 31
Yats

Aggie Cipolla — 34
Billy Boy's Blueberry Barn

Clay Robinson — 37
Sun King Brewery

John Ferree — 40
FarmIndy

Regina Mehallick — 43
R Bistro

Bud Koeppen — 46
Broken Wagon Bison

PASSION

Lali Hess — 52
The Juniper Spoon

Jeff Hawkins — 55
Hawkins Family Farm, HOPE CSA

Jesús Alvarez — 58
Lynethe's Deli and Pierogies

Barbara Sha Cox — 61
Indiana CAFO Watch

David Robb — 65
Harvestland Farm

Don Villwock — 67
Indiana Farm Bureau

Sonny Beck — 70
Beck's Hybrids

Jeff Simmons — 73
Elanco

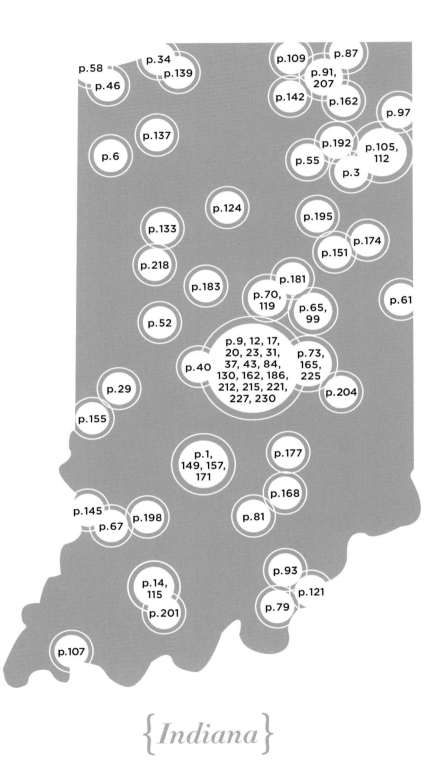

p.58
p.34
p.139
p.46
p.109
p.87
p.91, 207
p.142
p.162
p.137
p.97
p.6
p.192
p.105, 112
p.55
p.3
p.124
p.195
p.133
p.174
p.151
p.218
p.181
p.183
p.70, 119
p.61
p.52
p.65, 99
p.9, 12, 17, 20, 23, 31, 37, 43, 84, 130, 162, 186, 212, 215, 221, 227, 230
p.40
p.73, 165, 225
p.29
p.204
p.155
p.1, 149, 157, 171
p.177
p.168
p.145
p.81
p.67
p.198
p.93
p.14, 115
p.121
p.201
p.79
p.107

{*Indiana*}

ARTISANAL

Judy Schad — 79
Capriole Farmstead Goat Cheese

Tim Burton — 81
Burton's Maplewood Farm

Chris Eley — 84
Goose the Market, Smoking Goose

Greg Gunthorp — 87
Gunthorp Farms

Sharon Yoder — 91
Yoder Popcorn

Ted Huber — 93
Huber's Starlight Distillery

Max Troyer — 97
Sechler's Pickles

David Barrickman — 99
Wildflower Ridge Honey

STARTING OVER

Bernadette Olivier and — 105
Elie Laurent Apollon
Refugee gardeners

Bud Vogt — 107
Bud's Farm Market

Nick Boyd — 109
South Side Soda Shop and Diner

Gustavo Rodriguez and — 112
Yalili Mesa
Caliente Cuban Cuisine

Dave Fischer — 115
Fischer Farms

Lisa Sparks — 119
Lisa's Pie Shop

Warren and Jill Schimpff — 121
Schimpff's Confectionery

Maria Gonzalez — 124
Former migrant worker

THE GOODS

Marcus Agresta — 130
Piazza Produce

Kim Robinson — 133
Two Cookin' Sisters

Larry Wappel — 137
Wappel Farms

Carl Garwood — 139
Garwood Orchard

Scott Tucker — 142
Maple Leaf Farms

Mike Horrall — 145
Melon Acres

Jean Kautt — 149
Bloomingfoods

Mark Souers — 151
Ivanhoe's

Gary Morris — 155
Clabber Girl Corporation

Daniel Orr — 157
FARMbloomington

FAMILY

The Resler Generations — 162
Blue-ribbon competitors

Heather Hill — 165
Hill Farms

Lois Rust and Ruth Ann Hendrix — 168
Rose Acre Farms

Bill Oliver — 171
Oliver Winery

Darrell and Craig Brown — 174
Brown Family Farm

Misao and Clara Kurayama — 177
Satuma Japanese Restaurant

Colt Reichart — 181
Red Gold

The Shoup Family — 183
Shoup's Country Foods

Brent Joseph — 186
King David Dogs

BACK TO ROOTS

Dani Tippmann — 192
Miami Tribe

Doris Artis Walters — 195
Weaver Settlement descendant

Chris Vosters — 198
Wibs Stone Ground Grain

The Sisters of St. Benedict — 201
Simply Divine Bakery

Eleanor Arnold — 204
Oral historian

Elaine Jones — 207
The Carriage House

FUTURE

Sam Brown — 212
Second Helpings

Lisa Harris — 215
Eskenazi Health

Jay Akridge — 218
Purdue University College of Agriculture

Susanne Wasson — 221
Dow AgroSciences

Roy Ballard — 225
Purdue Extension, Hancock County

Thom England — 227
Ivy Tech Community College

Aster Bekele — 230
Felege Hiywot Center

About Indiana Humanities — 235
Acknowledgments — 237

PLACE

*"I don't think there's any other place where the same cast
of characters would cross paths."*

MARCIA VELDMAN

MARCIA VELDMAN

BLOOMINGTON COMMUNITY FARMERS' MARKET

Every Saturday morning, April through November, the parking lot of Bloomington's City Hall is turned into the state's largest farmers' market, with spaces for 100 vendors, live music, and special events like an annual heirloom tomato festival, where it's not unusual to find as many as thirty-five different types of the lovingly grown fruit. The market, which has been in existence at different sites since 1975, is managed by the city's Department of Parks and Recreation; Marcia Veldman has served as its coordinator since 1998. "I came back to Indiana to be a truck farmer," says Veldman. "I didn't even know I was interviewing to manage the market."

{ *Bloomington* }

Truly a crossroads

A number of different things come together beautifully here in Bloomington. The community support is just amazing. That's most evident to me on those early spring days when it's raining and it's cold.

There are customers shopping in the rain with umbrellas and trench coats. They really care about getting their food locally, about supporting small farmers. Over the years, it's become part of the culture of the community.

And because of the hills and hollows around here, people have been growing on small plots for a long time, whereas in other places there are big flat stretches of land turned to corn and soybeans. We didn't have as much opportunity for corn and soybeans here, so there's a long history of people putting out large gardens. Once they start selling at the market, some of those large gardens turn into small farms. I think that has really helped the market.

The market's also been managed from the beginning in a community-based way. It's open to anyone who grows what they sell in Indiana, which is kind of different from a lot of markets that, say, want thirty-five total vendors—and so many people with flowers. We're like, if you grow it, you are welcome to sell here.

Sometimes I think it's challenging for the vendors because you don't know from one year to the next how many people

"One of the things I think is really neat to see on a Saturday morning is the melding of the community, where the market is truly a crossroads."

are going to have tomatoes. But this really pushes the creativity and ingenuity of the vendors to look for those niches that other people aren't filling. You can see thirty different kinds of potatoes being sold. When you have a more controlled environment it's like, okay, these people are the potato growers and they might be satisfied with five varieties.

I think having professional management for the market is also beneficial. A lot of markets are volunteer based, which is wonderful, but having some consistency from year to year, having someone whose job it is to keep looking at the changing needs of the market has helped.

For example, we were the first open-air market in the state to allow for the sale of meat. It took a lot of time to work through the different agencies in the state, to get everybody on board and comfortable, to document how that can happen, and to make it happen. When you're a volunteer base or have very limited staffing, it's hard to take the time to make those kinds of things happen.

One of the things I think is really neat to see on a Saturday morning is the melding of the community, where the market is truly a crossroads. I don't think there's any other place where the same cast of characters would cross paths. It's a place where anyone can come and feel really comfortable and at home. That's unusual. You don't find a lot of places where very wealthy people and low income people or people who live in a certain neighborhood come together with people from the university.

I really feel it's hard to imagine Bloomington without the market at this point. There's this energy that spurs so much. People cross paths and start conversations about things happening in their neighborhoods. Those conversations might turn into a group that takes a stand on something. So it really engages the community in a way that's hard to do otherwise because so much of it is based on chance. You go to the market to buy your produce, then you're running into your neighbors, having those conversations.

It always blows my mind—leaving on a Friday night and it's this empty parking lot. Then, during the market on Saturday, it's this amazing, thriving place.

PETE AND ALICE ESHELMAN

JOSEPH DECUIS

The Joseph Decuis restaurant and emporium is a nationally recognized outpost of fine food and dining on a sawed-off main street in little Roanoke, a country crossroads southwest of Fort Wayne. Pete and Alice Eshelman moved to Roanoke over twenty-five years ago when Pete, a former professional baseball player who was drafted by the Yankees in 1976 and worked in the Yankees' front office, brought his sports insurance business here. What started as a way to entertain clients and colleagues became a public destination when the Joseph Decuis Restaurant opened in 2000. Since then, the enterprise has grown to include a farm, where much of the restaurant's food, including its Wagyu beef, is raised, the emporium—a casual café and retail store—and a bed and breakfast. The farm is also open to occasional tours and for special events featuring fine outdoor dining. As for Joseph Decuis, he is one of Pete Eshelman's Louisiana ancestors, a Revolutionary War veteran who went on to become one of the largest landholders in the state. Family tradition holds that Decuis's family never had a meal that wasn't served on a white tablecloth.

{ *Roanoke* }

The ultimate farm-to-fork experience

Pete: I think Indiana should become an international culinary destination, like Napa, like New York. Why can't we? We live in one of the great breadbaskets of the world. We've got a very distinct personality. We've got unique foods. We've got hospitality that I think is unmatched.

When we started Joseph Decuis, I told the staff, "We're going to start a restaurant." The way I was brought up was to be the best in the world at what you try to do,

whether it be with the Yankees, win the World Series, or in business. I said, "We're going to build one of the finest restaurants in the country."

Alice: And we all gasped. We're just starting out! It was a bigger vision than anybody else had.

Pete: About half the people believed it and half didn't. The half that didn't are gone. It was the entrepreneurial spirit. But it

was also a practical thing. We needed a place to entertain clients from around the world. Then my friends, who are business guys, embraced it, using it as their entertainment venue, and it just kind of grew.

Alice: Pete always used to say he'd love to own a restaurant one day. And I kept telling him that's 'cause you've never worked in a restaurant. That's how I earned my way through college; was working as a waitress over the summers. So ignorance

was bliss. But what happened was bringing people home, bringing guests home, and then starting as a corporate dining facility. He was the one who opened it to the public.

Pete: Then we started growing foods for the restaurant because, quite frankly, it was hard to find good foods at that time. Now you can; there are a lot of farms we're aware of.

We tasted the Kobe style Wagyu beef and that just blew our minds. That took me to Texas, Iowa, ultimately Japan. Our farm is now a full-blown Wagyu farm. You close your eyes, you could be in Hokkaido, Japan, where Mr. Takeda taught us the business. We also raise Mangalitsa pigs, which are from Austria and Hungary and marble the same way as Wagyu. Poulet Rouge chickens we get locally. So we like to feature unique things that we raise or are from other farms.

Alice: We start with good ingredients, but it's not grandma's cookin'. It's a takeoff on what you might get in New York or LA.

Pete: Mr. Shogo Takeda, the number one Wagyu farmer in Japan, is eighty-six years old now. He sent his U.S. representative three times before he would even meet with us to make sure we were for real. Finally, after the third time, he invited us to Japan. So my brother Tim and I went.

We were there for eight days. It was very important for him that we tour Japan and respect their culture. Then we met with him and we hit it off. He showed us his farm and advised us on what genetics and animals we should buy to start with. He also offered to be our teacher and to show us how to raise them because it's one thing to have the genetics, but it's another thing how you raise them. The Japanese way is stress-free, no drugs, no hormones. They have a tremendous respect for these animals. Then he came over and helped me design our facilities. He's been a real mentor.

Alice: He's become a part of our lives.

Pete: We give farm tours on Saturday from five to six, and then people dine afterwards. That's really the ultimate farm-to-fork experience. You get to see where your food is raised and how it's raised. You get to meet the owners and the farmer. Then you come here and enjoy it. I love doing that because you learn where people are coming from. I think there's a real curiosity and interest and passion. People are also worried about some of these food recalls and where their food comes from. Shrimp from Thailand? You've got to be kidding me. It's cheap, but how was it raised? What was in the water? I think consumers are getting a lot more interested in that. When I eat Wagyu beef, I want to taste the pure taste of that meat because I know thirty months went into that—and about 2,000 years to get it to that point.

The customer votes. If we're successful, that means a lot of people are coming to the restaurant. You're in the hospitality business to make people happy. I liken the culinary world to the Wild West. It just abounds with opportunity, and we are taking it to the next level.

GARY CORBETT

FAIR OAKS FARMS

On Interstate 65, just south of Merrillville, you'll find a sculptural replica of a black and white Holstein cow with a sign proclaiming, "A Dairy Good Time for the Family." This is the gateway to the Adventure Center at Fair Oaks Farms, one of the nation's largest dairy farms and a leader in agricultural tourism. Fair Oaks milks a herd of 30,000 Holsteins, fed a diet of alfalfa and corn silage, three times a day. Fair Oaks milks on twelve sites, covering 27,000 acres. The Adventure Center alone is 600 acres. There, visitors can see a 4-D movie (it splashes), take a train ride, and scale a milk-carton climbing wall. But they can also learn about how a large-scale dairy farm works by taking a guided tour of milking and processing facilities and watch a calf being born (about 120 calves are born at Fair Oaks every twenty-four hours). Fair Oaks produces a full line of dairy products, including butter, ice cream, and award-winning cheeses. Gary Corbett, Fair Oaks' CEO, greeted us in the work clothes he prefers: a ball cap and jeans.

{ Fair Oaks }

A cow's a terrific animal

Dairy is a complicated industry. It's the most regulated food in the United States. There's not even a close second. We are paid for our milk as to how it is used. Contrast that with a bushel of corn. If a bushel of corn goes into cow feed or if it goes into corn flakes, it costs the same. Doesn't matter what the end use is.

In dairy, it's entirely different. It absolutely matters what the end use is. If it goes into a bottle as fluid, that's the highest paid: milk. The next category is anything that can be eaten with a spoon: ice cream, cottage cheese, sour cream, yogurt. The third level is cheese, and the fourth is butter and powder. So we like to sell as much of our milk in the bottle as we can.

The southeast part of the United States doesn't produce nearly enough milk for itself, but it's got a lot of people who consume milk. Locating up here was a gateway to that market, which is virtually an all class-one market. Class one is a fluid market. So we could sit up here because this is a great place to produce milk and produce it cheaper and ship it to Florida than they can produce it down there because they fight some things: humidity and heat and water restrictions and a lot of other things, like feed availability.

What also struck us is that there's less than 2 percent of our U.S. population involved in agriculture. If you're of my vintage and didn't grow up on a farm yourself, you probably had an aunt or an uncle or a grandfather that you could go visit for a summer and at least understand a little bit about the smells and the sights.

We're three or four generations removed from that in the United States. Fifteen, twenty years ago, there were 300,000 dairy farms. Today, there are only 50,000. The numbers keep dwindling. Yet you can turn on the TV some nights and see these horror stories coming from agriculture because somebody snuck a camera in someplace. We are against those kinds of things as much as anybody is. They put agriculture in a bad light.

Most of agriculture has always taken the

"It's something that I think the world needs. You know, you've got the public out there that wants to re-identify with rural roots."

historical position that the world ended at the farm gate. A lot of farmers tend to be farmers because they are independent and don't want to associate with people. But this kind of created a perfect storm, where you have this huge reservoir of people that don't understand agriculture.

We made a conscious decision that we were going to take a different approach. Instead of being reactive to situations, we were going to try to become proactive. We made a decision that if we were going to stay in this thing, we would open our farms to the public.

In January 2004, we opened up this part of our business with the idea of being an edutainment center—to educate, hopefully, in an entertaining way and allow people to learn more about agriculture. We had three primary messages that drove everything we created: that agriculture and the environment are compatible; that agriculture and animal welfare are compatible; and that milk's good for you. It's been successful. We have 475,000 to 480,000 visitors a year.

We've gotten a lot of publicity, virtually all of it positive. "Dirty Jobs" [a Discovery Channel show] did a whole show from here. The Museum of Science and Industry in Chicago came down and, unbeknownst to us, did a couple of tours on their own, and then said they had a farm section in the museum but it was old and antiquated and would we redesign it? So now if you go to the Museum of Science and Industry and go to the farm section, you see Fair Oaks.

It's something that I think the world needs. You know, you've got the public out there that wants to re-identify with rural roots. Maybe they've heard that their grandfather or great-grandfather was a farmer. Then, too, more and more people are concerned about where their food comes from, food safety, and things that go along with that. We fill a void that's out there right now.

A cow's a terrific animal. You give it a hundred pounds of food and thirty gallons of water; it'll give you a hundred-plus pounds of milk. It will also give you a hundred-plus pounds of manure. That's an issue when you're as big as we are. You need to do something with it.

We didn't look upon that as an encumbrance. We looked upon it as an opportunity. So we harvest 100 percent of our manure in these huge vacuum cleaners. And we run 100 percent of our manure through anaerobic digesters. We create a biogas that's 58 percent methane. Anything electrical that you'll see today, wherever you go on these farms, we create it ourselves. We create 100 percent of all our own electricity. We create so much biogas that we have a lot of excess, way more than we need for electricity. We sell that back to the grid.

We can now scrub that biogas and make it about 99 percent methane, which is natural gas. Now we're compressing that natural gas and we're powering all of these big milk tankers that deliver sixty loads of our milk everyday to the southeast. Natural gas is powering all of our tractors.

It's not cheap. But it's doable. And it has a lot of payback, we feel, in the long run, because you're doing the right thing. We don't do a dairy now without a digester. We had to do a lot of adaptations as we tried it, because it had never been done quite to this scale, but I think it's something you'll see gain more favor as time goes on. It allows your neighbors to become a lot more hospitable because they know you're trying to do the right thing. We think it's the future.

LAURA AND TYLER HENDERSON

GROWING PLACES INDY

Laura and Tyler Henderson planted their first garden together while serving as house parents for a fraternity at Butler University. In 2004, they moved to Europe, where Tyler pursued graduate studies and Laura, a yoga instructor, taught classes. Upon returning to Indianapolis in 2006, the Hendersons became involved with the city's burgeoning slow food movement [Slow Food International works to provide good, clean, and fair food for all]. Laura founded the Indy Winter Farmers Market and, together, the Hendersons formed Urban Earth Indy, an initiative to create city gardens in association with such enterprises as R Bistro restaurant, Goose the Market, Invoke Yoga Studio, and Indiana Humanities. In 2010, Laura and urban farmer Matthew Jose created the Slow Food Garden, a 6,000-square-foot space at the city's White River State Park, which led to the establishment of Growing Places Indy, a nonprofit organization where both Laura and Tyler currently work.

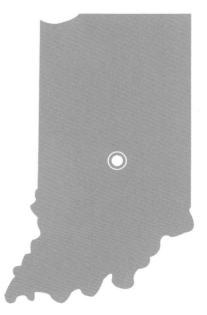

{*Indianapolis*}

There really is a food culture here

Tyler: My beginnings were incredibly modest. I gave zero consideration to what I was eating, how I was eating, how much I was eating, until I was in my mid-twenties. I thought there were only two kinds of apples—Red Delicious and Granny Smiths. Lettuce was iceberg. Peas came from a can.

When Laura and I moved to Europe, my culinary world really opened up. We lived in Norway and Finland, and I started to see that people there cared a lot more about food than anyone I'd been around.

I was twenty-seven and sort of disappointed in myself that I hadn't thought about this all along the way.

When we finished up in Europe, we had to decide whether to stay there or move back to the States and we decided to move back. We bought this house, and I was working as a consultant for a university in Italy, so I had a lot of free time and tried my hand at growing food in the backyard.

I realized I was learning to farm on a really small scale—three- or four-hundred square feet. I was constantly reading about soil health and environmental health, related to food.

I met Matthew Jose, who was doing Big City Farms, and I started wandering out there to help him as I had time. Through that we started to talk about what Big City Farms would look like if it could get big enough that I could be a partner and give up one of my office jobs.

All of a sudden I thought, "I have become a farmer!"

The urban context probably doesn't feel like farming to a lot of people, and, for a while, it didn't feel like farming to me. In my head, farming involved a tractor and a large field, a commodity crop, and, probably, animals. Then you think: We're actually growing food that people immediately eat.

That's a benefit of urban farming. You have all of these distractions that allow you to be less obsessed with the farm life. You can get on your bike and ride away from the farm and do something social.

That's something a lot of rural farmers tell us they're really envious of. At the same time, we're envious of their availability of space and their ability to have animals. I think it's a grass-is-greener situation.

Laura: My only brother was killed in a car accident in July 2004. This was just months before Tyler and I moved to Norway. That, of course, changed my life.

We had started doing a community garden with friends in Whitestown. We were out there the day of the accident, and that night, before we heard of the accident, we had dinner with some very dear friends. We talked a lot about food and what food means to peoples' lives. We even talked about the challenges of trying to cater a funeral. Then we got the news my brother had been killed. It took my world and exploded it into a million pieces.

It put me in a very reflective place, prompting me to explore life in a greater sense, as well as the practice of the physical body and what impacts its health. I found a lot of comfort in preparing food.

Tyler and I decided to do what we could to make this a place where we wanted to live as long as we're here. I opened the [Indy] Winter Farmers Market. But we felt there needed to be more opportunities for people in the city to connect with how food is grown without necessarily having to go to a farm. Farmers don't have all the time in the world to teach people about what they're doing.

Bob Whitt, director of White River State Park, approached Tyler and I and said they had this land and were interested in it being a garden: Would we look at it and see what we thought?

We had talked with Matthew Jose about how, in other cities, there are agriculture programs where people can participate and learn about farming, and we wanted to see something like that in Indianapolis.

It's a lot of fun because we connect not just with people who live in town but people who are visiting Indianapolis. For them it's a chance to see there really is a food culture here. I've been floored. There are days when it's hard to get anything done because so many people stop and ask questions. And as soon as you start telling them about it, you can almost see them going back to a space in time where they have some story about their childhood or their grandparents or the garden they used to have.

Everybody eats. No matter who you are. No matter where you come from. No matter how much money you have, you have to eat. It's part of our survival. So you can gather people from all walks of life around a garden, around food, and find something in common. I think that was part of the vision for that space, and it's proven to be true.

KAY GRIMM AND SUE SPICER

FRUIT LOOP ACRES

Farmers can be a lot like artists. They are creative risk takers who tend to do what they do because they can't imagine doing anything else. Kay Grimm happens to be an artist who also farms. Before she was growing food, Grimm was known as an installation artist whose specialty was making things from found objects. Then she discovered organic, locally sourced agriculture. For the better part of a decade, Kay, with her partner, Sue Spicer, have been building a market for goods produced by small, independent farmers, taking what amounts to a farmers' market on wheels to various Indianapolis neighborhoods. But perhaps Grimm and Spicer's most distinctive work is Fruit Loop Acres, the three-quarter-of-an-acre property, located in one of Indianapolis' toughest neighborhoods, that has become an outpost for their obsessions with art, fresh food, and nature.

{ *Indianapolis* }

Communing art and nature

Kay: When I started to get older, I wanted to work smarter, not harder. I had a seed company called Kids in Bloom: Living History Seeds. We used to do all our growing of heirloom seeds by trial and test, and it was a lot of work. It's not easy to grow lots of different seeds.

So I started planting in a permaculture type method, where things are interplanted. You create islands. You plant your mature, deciduous trees on the south side so you get your winter sun warmth and then the cool of the shade during the summer. I created all these little islands and they have matured into different habitat areas interlaced with fruit.

Sue: This yard has been quite an education from the way I was raised to look at tending a yard and food. Being with Kay these last eight years, I know a lot more about why I feel how I feel from the food I eat, the different external inputs. I've really been able to find a more secure happy place within myself through what we've done with our little environment and the high-quality, clean food we eat.

Kay: It's really hard to replicate nature because it's so artful. My take on combining art into nature is like a natural segue. It enhances the existing nature that's there. You're communing art and nature and I think that's the highest form of spirituality.

You're working with nature, not against it. That's the biggest rule of thumb.

Sue: It's an art park here; it's just not labeled.

Kay: We get to turn people on to fruit who didn't think you could grow fruit like that in the city.

Sue: Passion fruit. People still drop their jaws on that one.

Kay: And how phenomenal-tasting our black raspberries are.

Sue: I think part of the satisfaction is teaching people what real food tastes like.

Kay: The Sun King guys make beer from our fruit. Think how many hundreds of people get to try it.

That's what I like. Probably my best art yet is right here.

ALAN HANSELMAN

SCHNITZELBANK RESTAURANT

Jasper, Indiana, is a town of just over 13,000 people, founded in 1830. German roots are deep here, as are traditions of hard work and quality craftsmanship. Look closely and you'll actually see street signs that say strasse *after their assigned names. Serving traditional southern German cuisine, the Schnitzelbank Restaurant has been one of Jasper's top destinations since 1961, when it was started by Larry and Betty Hanselman. The place has been through several incarnations since then. Alan, one of six Hanselman children now involved in running the restaurant, is the manager.*

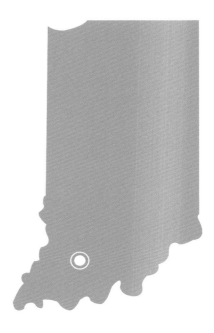

{*Jasper*}

Something no one else could do

Schnitzel means *a piece of.* The *schnitzel*—wiener schnitzel—means a piece of the *wiener* or the veal. The *schnitzelbank* is a carving bench. There is one that's sitting outside the restaurant, out front, and it's an actual *schnitzelbank*. We had to reinforce it because people take so many pictures and they sit on it.

Dad got started in 1961. He was big in softball and stuff like that, so he had a lot of friends. There was a tavern on this site, but people couldn't get it to go. He wanted to give it a shot.

He realized early on that every time a new place would start in town, all of his booze business would go down the street because they were selling it five cents cheaper. So he learned that it was the food that kept people coming back, something no else could do. This was a German area and he went to many of the local families and asked them to give their German recipes. That's where the recipes actually came from, was the locals around here. That's how he got his start.

In '71 they started tearing the original building down. It was the oldest building in Jasper and people started taking bricks out and were gold-plating them. Dad had to stop them because he was still open for business at the time and they were coming through the wall!

But in 1971 he started the new place, and

"That's where the recipes actually came from, was the locals around here."

two years later we had to add to it because it was just so popular. We added on to it one more time in 1988; we actually added another room on the front. So we built on to this three times since Dad started. Then we added a catering business, and we also have the hotel, the Hampton, that's right next-door.

I would say out-of-towners are our big draw. Over the years, we've become more of a tourist attraction because there are not very many German restaurants in the state of Indiana and we're still an independent restaurant. I think a lot of people look for those. I know I'm like that: If I go somewhere, that's the first thing I ask for. I want a local, independent place and not a chain.

We're really proud of our sausages. We developed them with a local meatpacker, Merkley's. They came in with us and made different kinds, and we finally got the taste we liked. That means you won't get these sausages anywhere else because they were made specifically for us. Almost everyone has had a bratwurst; that's our most popular sausage. But if you want to try something else, we'll talk you into a bockwurst. It's spiced a little bit differently.

And you've got to try the kraut balls. Everybody goes, "Oh, I don't like sauerkraut." Well, these don't taste like sauerkraut at all! They have a very unique taste.

I was out in Idaho, and a guy comes up to me and says, "Hey, I've been in your place." It's amazing to me how many people have been here. My oldest son is getting ready to come back; he'll be the third generation. It's become a proud family tradition to carry on. If you're ever over in Germany, families actually live in the same house together. The grandparents are upstairs, then the parents are on the middle floor, and the kids, who are running the business, are on the bottom. You see that a lot over there; I think maybe some of that's carried over here.

BECKY HOSTETTER

DUOS

A seemingly irresistible force in the Indianapolis food scene, Becky Hostetter, together with her husband, David, opened the city's first vegetarian restaurant, the beloved Essential Edibles, in the early 1990s. Since then, Chef Becky has served as a personal chef to the Irsay family (of Indianapolis Colts fame) and, most recently, with collaborator John Garnier, as coproprietor of the Duos food truck, a roving kitchen that promises to serve "slow food fast." She has been a witness to momentous changes in how Hoosiers think about food—and how food has helped transform her city.

{*Indianapolis*}

Creating a scene

Essential Edibles was a strictly vegetarian restaurant and, when we opened back in the 1990s, we were so guarded about that. We never promoted it as such. We just promoted it as good food, which is an obvious difference between then and now: It's not a shameful thing to say you offer vegetarian food! It's not as difficult to convince carnivores to give it a go.

I've been a vegetarian for almost forty years. It used to be in Indianapolis you could only go to a salad bar or an Italian place. When my in-laws took us out, we'd be like, "Where's the best salad bar we can go to?" It's very, very different now. I've noticed that chefs are letting vegetables be the star. I mean pork is a big star right now as well, which is a very good

Indiana thing to do. But people are realizing the potential of a good vegetable prepared properly.

I'm planning my menus more thoughtfully for the season. And for this particular business, where we're doing street food, there has to be a price point that works, while we try to offer as much local and seasonal product as we can. That's really been an interesting line to walk. We're working on it all the time.

You learn to network to help grow your base. I used to feel quite alone in trying to figure that out. That's not the way it is anymore. I mean everybody helps everybody find somebody. If tomatoes are tight this week, my tomato guy is helping me think who else is going to have them.

The food truck is also a community-building experience. Even though I didn't think I ever wanted a restaurant again, I liked the idea of setting up somewhere and creating a scene where people could interact with each other. I like that idea a lot.

And I like that our menu can change every week, being able to make what we feel like making. I think the price point is a really good thing for the consumers and for exposure to new foods. I hope that more ethnic restaurants will see it as an opportunity. People can't afford to get started in a brick-and-mortar structure. There's an African cook here, she has a business called Safari Kitchen. She's Kenyan. She has a little trailer but she hasn't hit the streets yet, and I'm like, "Oh, please!" It would be so lovely to see. I envision a little Indian truck, like I saw when I was in India a long time ago. That's when I started thinking about street food.

I think that's coming down the pike. It's a good way to broaden our culinary community with people who have a passion for cooking but can't afford a $100,000 build-out.

I have this whole thing about us being a city that we need to embrace and participate and be part of. That's really important to me. And I think food trucks can help create that sense of urbanism and vitality.

JANE AND FRITZ KUNZ

TRADERS POINT CREAMERY

Indiana's only organic dairy, Traders Point Creamery, is even more remarkable for being located within the Indianapolis metro area. Established by Jane and Fritz Kunz in 2003, Traders Point Creamery produces award-winning organic, grass-fed nonhomogenized dairy products including Creamline Artisan Ice Cream, which serves as basis for the amazing milk shakes served at the dairy's organic restaurant, the Loft. Traders Point Creamery provides farm tours and hosts a farmers' market, as well as nature hikes and a healthy kids program. "We've been fortunate in that almost every school district in the metropolitan area has been to Traders Point Creamery," says Fritz. "Their early memories of the first livestock that they've been close enough to touch might have been here at our farm."

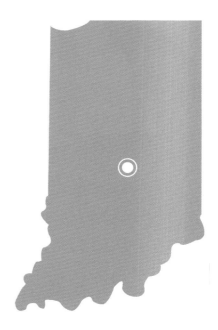

{Indianapolis}

It's been a rodeo at times

Jane: This was my grandmother's farm, and it was part of a dairy operation. So when we inherited this farm, we decided we wanted to continue that. But with Fritz being a doctor, we were also on board that what we put in our bodies should be organic, with no chemicals, and a healthful product.

In 1999, we went up to Wisconsin and studied Organic Valley farms and how they were doing; how much land they needed for rotational grazing because the rotational grazing was a very important part of the animals' health. That's what the cows were used to when they were originally bred. Eating grass is what their stomachs are all about and the grass-fed products give us lots of high CLA (conjugated linoleic acid), omega-3s, and immune system boosters.

Fritz: When Jane's grandmother died, her last request was, "Don't sell my farm." That was a big request. We thought this farm would be sold because it was so developable. But Jane's father really lived up to his mom's wishes. He was willing to let us take a stab at it. So it skipped a generation. We got the chance to invent this place because it was really just pastureland.

Jane: And we were bringing our kids along on this journey. We wanted to make sure it was a journey we would all be proud of. I can remember one day sitting on the porch over there at the barn thinking, we don't really own this land. We're caretakers. This is something we should look at as if it's not really ours, but it's something that will continue on, so how do we care for it?

Then we're in the city limits. It's really crazy.

Fritz: It's been a rodeo at times. We've

had to catch animals at three and four o'clock in the morning, with the police department helping chase them down the street. I'd drop bales of hay in the middle of a busy intersection as I'm rounding a corner, and I get home and think, didn't I have another one of those? I wonder where it is?

Certainly as far as traffic and moving farm equipment down the roads, that's going to be a problem for us. But we have access to a community of 1.2 million people for our products. That's a plus.

Jane: I think people appreciate the effort that we've put out and what we're trying to do. We are, obviously, more expensive than the big dairies, but this is what it takes to do what we're doing. I think that when people come out here they understand that it takes quite a bit of effort to make this product. Then I think the price point is more palatable. We've learned a lot of lessons. The restaurant, for example, wasn't part of the plan. But people are out here and they want to have the product, taste the product, eat the product.

Fritz: One thing the architect told me was, "This is really a special area. You should try to protect and preserve it." So as we were doing the creamery, we decided to try to make this area a rural historic district. There are only two others in the whole state of Indiana. But in July 2009, after five years and many hours and dollars spent, the National Parks gave us the Traders Point Historic District, allowing 2,500 acres of rolling countryside in metropolitan Indianapolis to be historically protected space. That was pretty exciting.

We're protecting history. But we're also incredibly interested in the future and the "green" revolution. We're saying, why can't the historic district also be the green district, promoting green activities that we're all hearing about and people who want to garden and make products and have them available to consumers? Maybe this could all help make a really lovely district for the metropolitan area. We can't be Silicon Valley. Let us utilize what we have: the incredible fertility that produces this special food. Instead of celebrating computer chips, why don't we make cow chips?

CINDY HOYE

INDIANA STATE FAIR

Every August, hundreds of thousands of Hoosiers converge on the Indiana State Fairgrounds on East 38th Street in Indianapolis. At night, residents on the city's north side can hear the fair train's whistle blow, as it carries folks back to the suburbs after a day visiting exhibits, taking rides on the Midway, looking at animals like "the world's largest boar," and eating lots and lots of fair food. Over the years, Presidents Wilson, Franklin D. Roosevelt, Kennedy, Clinton, and George W. Bush have all made visits, as have Elvis and the Beatles. Cindy Hoye grew up just ten minutes from the fairgrounds. She and her family have lifelong memories of the place. In fact, her father won first prize in the Better Baby competition at the Better Baby Building in 1924. "There's something about the experience that generation after generation passes along," says Hoye.

{*Indianapolis*}

Deep-fried Twinkies

If you think of food, it doesn't start from the grocery store or the restaurant. It starts from the land. The fair's about the land, about growing and harvesting and producing agriculture. That's what we're here for: to showcase agriculture, youth, education.

I've been in the fair business for almost thirty years. When I started out in the fair business, especially here, the number one reason people came to the fair was for the animals. Number two [was] the exhibits. And number three was food. Now, it's turned out to be the number one reason why people come.

This fair is fascinating. It's the sixth-oldest state fair in the country, dating back to 1852. It's fun to look at some of the old photos of the food stands way back when. I remember growing up as a kid, there were long trailers and they had stools all the way around. There was a concession that was frying your hamburger and your onions and then counters, almost like a deli but portable. That was the style.

Food started out as just part of the culture of the fair.

I think it kind of started with the deep-fried Twinkies. Then we embraced it, and each year there's a signature-food dish competition. The concessionaires come up with different ideas, whether it's deep-fried macaroni and cheese or some

"It's the best milk shake in the world."

kind of product that features the commodity we're showcasing for the year. That whole deep-fried movement really caught on and changed why people come to the fair. It's interesting how that jumped ahead.

Two years ago, we said we've got to give people more options when they come here. Yes, the novelty food is fun and people like the deep-fried something-on-a-stick. At the same time, there are people that want some healthier options. So we shifted one of the concessions in the Agriculture Horticulture Building to healthier choices.

Not very successful.

But this past year, we ramped it up even more and said we're going to put a fresher face on it. We renovated the stand. We took a new approach to marketing. They had salads and they had strawberries; they had deli sandwiches, fat-free smoothies. I mean, all those kind of things. It was the year of soybeans, and we did tofu, too.

And the gross at the concession stand still wasn't where it should be.

So I think people want to know the choices or options are there, but I still believe people want to just come to the fair and check out for the day and say, "I'm going to have the fully fat something or other, because this is my one day where I can take a break and it's okay."

What's unique to us and special about the Indiana State Fair is years and years and years ago this fair decided they really needed to showcase the end products for the commodities: pork, beef, lamb, and then poultry. They set up these great big tents to provide pork chop sandwiches or a pork chop dinner. Volunteers staff them, run them. And it provides the revenue stream they need to run their organizations. The pork tent and the beef tent are part of what makes the Indiana State Fair more unique than the Ohio State Fair or any other fair. The farmers have raised the hogs and are the ones serving you the product.

If you were coming to the Indiana State Fair and you said, "What should I eat? I've one thing to buy. What should I buy?" I would buy one of the commodities. I would go to the Dairy Bar and have a milk shake. It's really like soft ice cream. It's the best milk shake in the world. They also have great grilled cheese sandwiches—all different varieties. Oh, my gosh, it's wonderful.

The Beef Cattle Association does rib eyes, and they're fantastic. We have a concessionaire that does Indiana lamb kebobs, and lamb burgers. … If I had to pick, depending on the day, it would be one of those commodities, because you can't walk into a restaurant and buy that milk shake or that pork chop dinner like you can during the fair. It's the ambiance that goes with it and the fact that the farmer is providing that food to you. There's something special about that experience.

RISK

"I wasn't trying to be brave, I just couldn't think of anything else to do."

BUD KOEPPEN

MIKE ROE

BRIDGETON MILL

Mike Roe loves history and knows how to make things. He's a skilled cabinetmaker who once dreamed of owning a water-powered cabinet shop. That's what kept drawing him to the historic Bridgeton Mill in Parke County. You could say the mill cast a spell on Roe. As he went through the process of bringing it back to life, he was also learning to become a miller. Now the mill, which first opened in 1823, produces over forty stone-ground, 100 percent natural products that are ground, hand mixed, and bagged on site by the Roe family.

{*Bridgeton*}

Actually a miller now

We had heard about the Covered Bridge Festival but had never been to it. My wife said, "Let's go…" and we came around this corner and I saw it: a covered bridge with the waterfall and the old mill on the hill.

After that, I'd swing by, see the old mill. Usually, there was nobody else around, which I thought was strange; it's such a beautiful sight.

Stopped by in '94 and there was a For Sale sign nailed to the front of the building. I came inside, and people were actually running it. I asked, "How much are you wanting for it?" and they told me. So I went outside, looked around, came back in, and said, "I'll take it." To me, it was like seeing a state park for sale.

The mill was in pretty bad shape. The floors were sagging. Back in the corner, it actually bounced when you walked on it because the termites had ate up so much underneath.

But I bought it and the family introduced themselves. They said, "Come on inside. We're going to teach you how to run this place." And I said, "Well, there's a good idea." Some of the equipment is 200 years old, you know.

I asked where we put the corn in. They said, "No, no, no, no. We got to take it all apart first." The stones are 200 years old. They weigh over 2,000 pounds. We had to pull them apart. Clean everything. Clean the ceilings, the walls, everything. We go downstairs and there're big old flat belts. There're the fly wheels, six feet tall, made out of wood.

Finally, we put in a bag of corn. So we're grinding and grinding, and we're talking

"So I went outside, looked around, came back in, and said, 'I'll take it.'"

about grandpa's recipes and the proper order of the mixing and the sifting, and the grinding.

They walk away, and I'm standing up there, grinding by myself. I thought, "What in the world are they doing now?" About that time, it ran out of corn.

Well, the two stones started rubbing together. So I raised the stone up and shut it off real quick. And they said, "You're going to be a pretty good miller!" They handed me the keys, and out the door they went.

Ernest Weise was German and trained in Germany as a miller. He came to the United States and worked in two or three different mills. Then he and his wife, Mildred, bought this place in 1940. We've reduced the amount of salt, but other than that we now make Ernest Weise's recipes and expand on that by using old Indian corns and organic corns.

What I'm trying to do is find the very best grains I can, wherever they're from. Buckwheat is the grain I get from Indiana. It comes from northern Indiana, and it's very hardy. My rye comes from Iowa. My wheats come from Montana. They're naturally white and very high in protein. I also get blue corn from Missouri, red corn from southern Mexico, and purple corn from South America.

This stone is a French buhr, which means it's the best stone ever made for grist mills. It's fresh water quartz, harder than glass. It has an estimated life of 300 years. Now, stones around here were very hard, like granite, but they would wear slowly away, which left a little gravel dust in your flour. These don't wear away. You have a much cleaner flour, better tasting.

Back before screens were invented [to sift or filter the grain], they used different grades of cloth and the cloth came in a bolt, so they called it bolting. Your four grades of cornmeal were corn flour, bolted, unbolted, and grits. Unbolted corn flour is our bestseller. It's old-fashioned cornmeal, whole grain. I get people spoiled on it. They have to come back here because they can't get it anywhere else.

I am actually a miller now. I think I'm just one of the luckiest guys in the whole world to able to recognize this old mill for what it was and what it could be. Look out that window: a covered bridge with a waterfall under it. I mean, how many people get to look out a window at that every day?

JOE VUSKOVICH

YATS

"I always say I fell and landed on the best corner in the world," says Joe Vuskovich, the owner of Yats, Indianapolis's hometown chain of Cajun-Creole restaurants. When Vuskovich, a native of New Orleans, arrived in Indy over ten years ago, he was in need of a fresh start. But the city was just as ready for Vuskovich's no-frills take on Cajun-Creole cuisine, not to mention his handmade approach to doing business. Within a year, the first Yats (New Orleans slang that, roughly translated, stands for an everyday person) at College Avenue and 54th Street on the city's north side was a word-of-mouth destination that was even being written up in the New York Times. *Since then, additional Yats locations have taken hold, and Vuskovich, whose generosity with customers and causes is legendary, has become one of the city's most celebrated hosts.*

{*Indianapolis*}

A taste of something different

My family was in the fishing business in New Orleans. My father was an oyster grower. He had a great reputation and survived the Depression because he had an exceptional product.

I knew early on that I didn't want to be a fisherman. But I had a brother who was a fisherman and he suggested to me, after I got out of the service, that we open an oyster bar.

I had never worked in a restaurant—I hadn't even eaten in too many restaurants. I was a kid; I was nineteen.

So we started a place in New Orleans with an oyster counter and four tables. It was an instant success. Eventually it grew to 700 seats. The name of the place was Visko's and next door, across the driveway, was a restaurant called The Steam Room (it was just steamed seafood) and then we had a third area that was a banquet facility and another bar that we called the Commissary. It was three places connected by patios and walkways. It all worked very, very well.

I was in the right place at the right time,

had old recipes that belonged to my mother and family, plus great employees, old time Cajun cooks, and people who cared about food and knew what they were doing. I learned a lot, was self-taught, and paid a lot of tuition because I made a lot of mistakes in business. But I learned.

Then the economy went down the drain. The oil boom bottomed out in the mid-eighties. People were driving cabs who had owned limousines.

When I was a kid there were places you

could go and get a plate of food for fifty cents. Corner grocery stores always sold sandwiches or had a pot of food going. It was fast food before there was fast food. I wanted that kind of neighborhood deal where you could pop in and things were ready to go.

My mother was a great Sicilian cook and my father, being a fisherman, he'd have Cajuns during the busy seasons, and they would cook big jambalayas and always have a pot of red beans on. You had to cook for a bunch of people, workmen on a boat.

My wife and I stopped in Indianapolis on our way to Chicago. We took a walk downtown, met some people, and decided this was a good place. It was small enough to feel like a hometown but big enough to have opportunities.

One night we went to see what Broad Ripple was like. We were driving past the corner of College and Fifty-fourth and saw this building. We pulled over, and I looked inside and said, "This place should be selling my food."

The place happened to be available. The guys who owned the space should not have let me rent it because I was broke at the time. The rent was so reasonable—way, way below market value. It was a blessing. That's why I remain grateful to these people and to this neighborhood. It took me forty years to realize this,

but I'll never do a business where I wouldn't live myself.

We had no advertising budget. We had no sign. We had a sign propped up against an automobile that said, "OPEN FOR LUNCH." We did eleven dollars the first day. Breaking a hundred dollars took us forever.

Then it started.

High school kids were some of our first customers. We don't sell booze because I like serving kids. They're your next generation. They're going to grow up and bring their kids. I like having a place where kids in high school can go and they're not eating hamburgers and typical fast food. They get a taste of something different and they can afford it. They can hang out and I don't mind it. I can expose them to Frank Sinatra, Tony Bennett, and all the old jazz that we play. Eventually they see their parents or their parents' friends coming in. They're in a social atmosphere where they can be pretty independent.

I tell our guys the restaurant has its place in society in the sociological order of things. I didn't realize it when I was a kid, but as I'm older I realize much, much more how what we do isn't just serving food. People might have invented the wheel a whole lot sooner if they'd had a restaurant around there someplace.

AGGIE CIPOLLA

BILLY BOY'S BLUEBERRY BARN

Indiana's blueberry country runs along the southeastern edge of the Lake Michigan coast. This is where U-pick farms, like Billy Boy's Blueberry Barn in Michigan City, abound. On the day we talked with Aggie Cipolla, who runs Billy Boy's with her husband, Bill, three or four families meandered through the rows of seven-foot bushes, pulling off the indigo berries and dropping them into coffee cans. It's a ritual shared by generations.

{*Michigan City*}

Mother Nature is the boss

My husband, Bill, grew up in a housing project in Chicago and always wanted a farm. He had a real estate book; he was always looking for places and, one day, he comes to me while I'm on the treadmill and he says, "I found something kind of interesting."

And I said, "Oh, great! What did you find?"

"I found a farm."

"Good."

And he says, "It's a blueberry farm."

I'm like, "Are you crazy?!"

I grew up in Rockford, Illinois, which is outside of Chicago. And I did have some relatives that were in farming. Also, my paternal grandparents in Sicily had a farm. But that's as far as it got.

The day we came to see this place, it was not pretty. It was very misty and drizzling and nothing was here. Meanwhile, Bill's getting happier and happier. He's getting excited. And I'm like, "You're going to do this, aren't you?"

He goes, "Eh, they're not going to take the bid."

And then they did. They did!

The first year we commuted every day from Chicago. We had no place to stay. All that was here was the barn and the little farm stand. There wasn't much business.

I had no idea how we were going to manage. But I started meeting people and I love being outside, so, after awhile, it seemed like this was not too bad.

We had never been blueberry pickers.

"We had never been blueberry pickers."

I always took my kids apple picking, strawberry picking, and never really realized about blueberry picking. The customers have taught me. They've taught me that this is something they do every year.

Our season usually starts between the fourteenth and the eighteenth of July because we have a later variety of blueberry. That's something else we didn't know: There are lots of varieties of blueberries! We have seven, including Bluecrops, Jerseys, and Bluerays. People have their tastes. They want the early ones, which are larger. We try to tell them those only last so long, so if you want them, they're not going to be here in August. They'll be smaller, but that variety is more intense in taste. They're very good; it just takes more time to pick them.

These blueberries need a balance: so much rain, so much sunshine. They have to have sandy, acidic soil. It's Mother Nature, you know? She's the boss. She decides. Last year, even though it was hot and we had enough rain, the last variety of blueberry never ripened. That's Mother Nature again. When you see them, buy them or pick them because you may not see them again until next year. They freeze wonderfully.

The biggest joy is seeing the families come back. The grandparents with the grandchildren; all the little kids. We get a lot of people here from all walks of life. It's nice to hear their stories. There's a family today on their way to Ohio—their friends told them to come here. They'd never picked before, so that's kind of fun.

A lot of our extended family come out, a lot of our friends come, too. It's nice because we get to visit with them. One of the girls who's worked here the longest gets excited because she says Billy Boy's is such a happy place. She kind of stopped me dead one day when I was stressed out about something. She goes: "Aggie, it's just so happy here."

And she's right!

CLAY ROBINSON

SUN KING BREWERY

In 2009, brewers Clay Robinson and Dave Colt opened Sun King Brewery, the first full-scale production brewery to operate in Indianapolis since 1948. Their plan was to sell 1,000 barrels of beer in their first year; they beat that number by a factor of five and almost doubled that a year later. Sun King's handcrafted seasonal and specialty beers are now available on tap and in cans throughout central Indiana. The Sun King phenomenon reflects a larger, statewide love affair with craft beer; close to forty brands are now in business. Today's brewers are recovering an Indiana tradition dating back to the utopian community of New Harmony, where the state's first significant brewery was created in 1816.

{Indianapolis}

I lost that bet

I started brewing in the spring of 1999. I'll never forget the first time I smelled the grain hit the hot water and that initial release of aromatics from the mixing of the mash. I was kind of baffled by how it all worked, but seeing that process made me want to know as much, learn as much, and work as hard as I possibly could because after I did it once, I never wanted to do anything else.

Working with beer is one of those things where you can be really creative. The brewing process is the same, but there are new types of hops that come out, new types of malting; there are new flavors that can be formulated, new styles of

beer cropping up all the time. There's this never-ending source of entertainment. Even though it's the same thing day in and day out, it's never the same.

To this day, a lot of the interest in craft beer comes from people brewing beer at home because people who brew beer tend to be very passionate about it. It's a really awesome thing to do. And, like anything else, you want to have people over and share it with them.

John Hill, who started the original brewpub in Indiana, Broad Ripple Brewpub, in 1990, was a home brewer. He was from England and worked his ass off to lobby

and work with the state government to change the law and make owning a brewpub legal. It's amazing that what I do to make a living, what employs upwards of seventy people, was illegal in Indiana twenty-two years ago.

Dave Colt and I have been making beer in downtown Indianapolis for the last twelve-to-fifteen years. The Sun King story goes way back because, as a brewer, one of the things you do is be social with people. You've got a whole list of people working in a pub, you're working right in and amongst everyone all the time, walking in and out of rooms, stopping and talking to people.

> *"It's amazing that what I do to make a living, what employs upwards of seventy people, was illegal in Indiana twenty-two years ago."*

I think a lot of the success of Sun King is tied to our roots in the community. I delivered most of our beer for the first six months, and every back door that I went through, there was either a bartender, a server, a host, or a cook that I had worked with over the last decade. That's part of why we wanted to be downtown. That's where the people who came to drink our beer knew us. I've lived in Indianapolis my entire life. I think it's a great city, I've seen it go through so many changes. Our goal was to be Indianapolis's brewery, and you really can't be Indianapolis's brewery if you're out in the suburbs or off by an industrial park or the airport. You really need to be downtown.

The whole reason we have a tasting room is because production brewing can be a very lonely environment. Nobody comes to see you in a production brewery; it's like a factory. But having a tasting room allows people to come in and actually smell the smells and see the sights and watch people work—to be engrossed in the brewery. When you come to Sun King, you are entrenched in the brewery environment. You're listening to whatever our brewers are listening to; you're watching people work and sweat. There's pumps going, there's canning lines operating, there's all sorts of sensory overload happening and, at the same time, everyone is happy to be here and enjoying themselves.

It's been great and interesting to see—especially over the past three or four years—people's attitudes change about the local movement. To see the rise of the Indy Winter Farmers Market and to see how many people come out Wednesdays to the downtown farmers' market and then, all of the different satellite markets. It's really nice to see a bunch of people in their late twenties, into their thirties and forties: this generation of us. Some of them have left and come back to do what they want to do here, and I think there's actually a lot more opportunity now. For so long we were just a corporate proving ground for restaurants and ideas.

There's definitely a huge shift in what people are supporting. I thought, at this point in time, I would still be going bar to bar with samples of beer and saying, "I'm Clay. I'm with a little local brewery and would you be interested in carrying local beer?" That's what I thought would happen.

But between the rise of people really caring about local, the rise of craft beer across the nation, and, my favorite, the rise of social media giving people the ability to communicate very easily and rapidly via Facebook and Twitter, we sold 5,000 barrels of beer our first year. When I wrote the business plan for Sun King, my five-year goal was to sell 5,000 barrels of beer.

I have to find a tattoo artist because Dave and I, when we were discussing whether we could sell 5,000 barrels of beer in a year (this was before we even named the business Sun King) I said if we could sell that many, I would get the brewery's name tattooed on my body. I don't have any tattoos, so it's a big step. I've never had anything I felt passionate enough about to want it permanently inked on me. But I feel that passionate about Sun King—because I lost that bet.

JOHN FERREE

FARMINDY

Seldom Seen is an old family farm John Ferree's grandfather acquired from his great uncle in trade for end-of-life care in the 1950s. According to Ferree, farming then skipped a couple of generations in his immediate family before he took it up, starting Seldom Seen Farm in Danville in 2004. In 2007, Ferree and his farming partner, Kelly Funk, were married. They ran the farm together until the summer of 2010 when Kelly was directly struck by a bolt of lightning while preparing for a weekend market. While Kelly's health has stabilized since the accident, she remains permanently disabled from the injuries she suffered.

When we met John, Seldom Seen had recently formed an alliance, FarmIndy, with Todd and Kathleen Jameson's Balanced Harvest Farm. The basis of FarmIndy is a community-supported agriculture (CSA) subscription plan featuring customized weekly shares of certified naturally grown produce, including heirloom and gourmet vegetables, fresh harvested and available with flexible payment plans. "We're hoping to make it more customer driven than farm oriented," says Ferree.

{*Danville*}

This is not a hobby

I had done a fair bit of traveling. Never graduated college. Opted to jump from place to place. Hitchhiked across the country and found a job in Milwaukee working on a 140-foot, three-masted schooner. Spent a season doing that.

A longtime friend of mine had rented an old farmhouse out here. It was like, "Hey, I'll just move back there. That's the next easiest thing."

Lived here for a couple of years and went, "You know, I'm commuting into Indy.

With the money I'm putting out in gas, surely I can do better on my own growing something."

I spent a year doing research. Settled on vegetable farming and did an internship in Champaign-Urbana. Then started up on my own. You know, when I started my own operation, I was twenty-five, so I was one of the younger ones when I got in the business.

It was a leap, I guess. But as far as a level of engagement that you work with on a

daily basis, this is much more challenging to me than it would be sitting in an office and simply being told what to do. I'm sure that's a pretty black-and-white view of it, but the fact of the matter is that I'm thirty-three. I have a lot of independence in what I do. No, I'm never going to get rich doing this, but what I do is rewarding to me. It's stimulating.

You never know what's coming the next day. Sailing, I felt like I learned more in nine months than I'd ever learned in my

"No, I'm never going to get rich doing this, but what I do is rewarding to me."

life. Farming, I spent nine months doing it and walked away thinking I didn't learn a damn thing until I started my own operation.

I think there are a lot of people trying to get in this that don't have that vision of how it can work. You know, I didn't feel like I had my head wrapped around what I was doing for three years. We made money and we put out product, but I didn't have a good handle on the business side of it, simply seeing production systems in use, marketing volumes, and having some idea of the financial side of it for probably three years. So that's the learning curve.

I'm saying this as somebody who got into it to be a reasonably scaled vegetable farmer. This is not a hobby. This is not something that I do for fun. It is not always pretty. It is not always easy. You are cold. You are miserable at times. You have to work when you don't want to work because that's simply what is demanded of you.

Indianapolis was pretty open. The farmers' markets were pretty open at that point in time. There weren't a whole lot of people doing it. There weren't a whole lot of people working with restaurants. That was helpful. I did have some start-up capital from what should have gone to my college education and that enabled me to buy some equipment, put up a greenhouse and basically set the stage for everything else. Outside of that start-up money, we've capitalized off our annual sales.

I think there's a level of quality we've committed to producing consistently. We've developed a pretty reasonable system where it actually comes together. There's no science that can make that happen.

The science side of it is simply being a competent grower, doing your homework, knowing what bugs you're going against, what diseases you've got to battle with, and finding techniques to deal with them, as well as calculating fertilization rates or potential yields. Figuring out why your potential yields didn't add up, why the spreadsheet didn't match reality.

We introduced the CSA about three years ago. It hasn't revolutionized how we do things, but it has brought a lot of security to our operation. On the business side, having the consistent volume going out every week. It would basically be like a corn guy selling a thousand acres of corn on contract. That is a known quantity. The market may go up or down and we may have rain on Saturday, but in the end, we've got the CSA to rely on.

We're going to start doing more farm events so that we actually have some face time. That's one of the big disadvantages to CSA. I have CSA members I've never met and that's not right.

The chefs that I have worked with I've liked very much. Working with Ryan Nelson or Greg Hardesty, that's fun. Tyler Herald at Patachou. I've worked in quite a few kitchens and speak the language. It's something I find rewarding. It's saved my butt. And then to go into a restaurant and eat what you've grown, I mean that's a good Saturday night.

Being done at the end of the day is my greatest source of pleasure. And actually having an intelligent, articulate crew that's fun to work with. Keeps you on your toes. Overall, it's the whole system, maintaining a small farm most people would probably view as marginal or eccentric and making it fly on a day-to-day basis. The challenge never ends. Sometimes you want it to. What else would I do? I don't know: Get a real job.

REGINA MEHALLICK

R BISTRO

Chef Regina Mehallick's award-winning R Bistro restaurant, on Massachusetts Avenue in Indianapolis, has provided diners with an ever-changing, highly focused menu of locally sourced, seasonal dishes for more than ten years. Trained at Johnson & Wales University in South Carolina, Mehallick worked extensively in the United Kingdom, serving as sous chef at the Yorke Arms in North Yorkshire, England, where she helped develop the celebrated country inn's contemporary take on British cuisine. A fierce advocate for independent restaurants, Mehallick has helped pave the way for a richer, more diverse restaurant scene in Indiana's capital city.

{Indianapolis}

Bringing people back

We came to Indianapolis from the U.K. in January 2000 so that my husband, Jim, could take a job with Cummins. It was really cold and snowy, but after two or three months I was settled in and decided to find a job.

Well, I couldn't find any independent restaurants. I didn't know what was going on. It seemed like there was this place called Broad Ripple, where there were a few restaurants, and then there was the north side, but we live off Southport Road on the opposite end of town, and I

didn't want to travel that far every day.

We ended up going to dinner at the Canterbury. It was a small restaurant within a small hotel, and I got a job there—but it wasn't ideally what I was looking for and, during that time, I was looking for spaces.

Where we lived was the suburbs, even though we were in Indianapolis, and I just didn't know much about the area. Chatham Arch, Lockerbie, the Old Northside—these were places I was unfamiliar with, not being a native. All I knew

was that I didn't want to be in a strip mall.

There was a gallery walk on Massachusetts Avenue in October of 2000. We didn't go on Friday night because, of course, I had to work. But on Saturday morning we came and were talking to one of the shop owners who said there was some space available here in this building. So we looked at it, I put some money down, an architect did a build-out, and we opened in May of 2001.

I was influenced by the years I worked in England, as well as when I was in Charleston, South Carolina. I wanted to

"What am I, a matriarch? Oh God, I don't know about that!"

have a really small menu that would capture all the major food components you would need. So there had to be a meat, a fish, a vegetarian, a poultry; and since we are here in the heartland, I thought we needed a comfort food. Comfort meals were just on the cusp on being trendy. And I definitely thought we needed to cater to vegetarians because it always seemed like they were left out in the cold. I sure as heck wasn't going to give them a plate of vegetables as their main course!

At the restaurant where I worked in England, we changed some of the dishes daily. Then, after a couple of years, there were things that were tried-and-true and were on all the time. I thought that's what I would do. But after I started, time went by, and I liked the variety of having a changing menu. I think the customers liked it, too. And I thought, "Wow, this is bringing people back."

Something else I learned while I was living in Europe was the fact that people over there eat much more seasonally than we do here in the United States. It's because of our grocery stores. You know, you can get asparagus for Christmas and that sort of thing, which is really not the rhythm and flow of the way life should be. Right now, we're in the bounty of summer; you should be having every fruit and vegetable that's growing in Indiana. So that also became part of my philosophy—that we should eat seasonally—and I factored that into the menu.

As far as desserts, I knew people loved chocolate, but I'm not a big chocolate dessert gal. I knew Elizabeth Garber from the Best Chocolate in Town and, since I didn't want to make chocolate truffles myself, I thought: What if I have her make dark and milk chocolate truffles, then people will have that chocolate craving satisfied. We've sold a tremendous amount of those truffles! That's been a good thing that's solidified her and my business arrangements. We support each other pretty strongly. I even influenced her to come to this end of Mass Ave when the space became available.

I also have a cheese plate. This was something that was pretty foreign to me when I moved to the U.K., but I saw that it was on menus all the time. So I wanted to end our menu with a little savory, as well as a sweet component and, surprisingly, it sells. That's a positive step that I think made the Indiana diner a little more savvy. It just opened them up to a nontraditional dessert.

In 2005, I went to a national meeting of women chefs and restaurateurs in Louisville, Kentucky. I was really surprised by how many independent restaurants and small farms they had in that state. I envy that, but we're coming around. I think that right now we're having an explosion of new, small independents. We need a lot more, but I think it's evolving. Now that I've been here for ten years, I guess I'm like, old. What am I, a matriarch? Oh God, I don't know about that!

BUD KOEPPEN

BROKEN WAGON BISON

Outside of Hobart, in northwest Indiana, you may find yourself slowing down at the sight of a grazing herd of bison. Bison are an iconic American animal; one even appears on the Indiana state seal. But the last free-roaming wild bison in Indiana was killed in 1830. Now Indiana bison ranchers like Bud Koeppen and his brother, Wally, are having a hard time keeping up with the demand for naturally low-fat, nutritionally rich bison meat. This demand has also led to growing stocks of animals once considered nearly extinct. "If you want to see more of them," says Bud, who rehabilitated wild animals before he started raising bison, "eat them. Because if you're eating them, somebody will raise them. If I wasn't selling meat, there wouldn't be eighty-three animals out there now."

{Hobart}

Wild streak

We give them four things to make them happy: We give them food, we give them water, we give them minerals, and we give the bulls cows. That keeps them happy. If one gets out, you don't have a problem. One won't leave, they're too herd-oriented. They'll want to get back in. But if they all got out, then you'd have a big problem. They might be ten miles away come morning.

They look slow and cumbersome, but they are very fast. They can spin on a dime on their front feet or their back feet. If you invade their private space, they're either going to flee or they're going to fight.

We know our individual animals. We kind of know which ones we can expect this from. We have one named Cruella de Vil. She's our best cow. She has calved every year. But you don't crowd her. She could have all the room in the world to flee—I mean there could be forty acres behind her, but if you approach her, she's going to take offense.

I can tell you how Cruella got her name.

She's one of the first cows we bought. In 2003, we bought seven bred cows, two young heifers and a breed bull who was only about eighteen months and weighed about 900 pounds. When we first got them, we put them in the corral for four days. We keep them there so they can get used to us and used to each other.

If, God forbid, the whole herd ever gets out, we can hopefully lead them back by showing them our grain pans. These grain pans are big and they're made of rubber.

Well, some pans were in the corral and along the fence. Nobody'd picked up the pans yet that day. Hadn't had the

"I wasn't trying to be brave; I just couldn't think of anything else to do."

opportunity; the animals were too close. There was one animal standing on the other side of the fence. This was January. It was four o'clock and getting dark and I figured that was a yearling heifer. I didn't look at her that close. So I climbed over the fence, picked up one pan, two pans, and headed for the third pan.

She was maybe twenty-five feet away and she turned and just looked at me. I seen her tag number: It was 1330. And I knew that was a bred cow. I go, "Oh!" I had nowhere to go. I said, "I'll just back out of here, I'm approaching you way too close." I moved one foot backwards … and she charged.

I had the two empty pans in my hands and I went, "Hunnnh!" I held them over my eyes and made a big noise, and she stopped, like ten feet away. Her eyes were locked on me. Her tail went straight up like a question mark. She was pawing the ground and wouldn't break eye contact with me.

I scolded her. "You behave yourself! You stay there! Don't you come any closer!" I'm holding the pans up and shaking my finger. I did that for fifteen or twenty seconds. Then I started backing out of there. And I got about twenty-five feet away again and she charged again.

I did the same thing. Again she stopped about ten feet away.

They're way faster than we are. They can get up to thirty-five, forty miles an hour. If she'd kept coming, I probably would have tried to bounce a pan off her head, dodge her at the last second. Whether or not that would have worked, who knows? I wasn't trying to be brave, I just couldn't think of anything else to do.

I scolded her and started backing up a second time. She let me back up. After I got about fifty feet away, her tail went down and she went about her business. And that's how she got her name: Cruella de Vil, the meanest old lady I could think of at that time.

The animals never come inside; they're never indoors. They'd as soon have it zero out than they would have it be ninety. There's a saying among bison producers: You got a sick animal, you got a dead animal. By the time you know it, it's too late. They're used to hiding the fact they're sick until the very last minute because if they show it in the wild, the wolves or the grizzlies are going to pick on them. They're the ones that get singled out. So they have to conceal the fact they're not feeling well. And even if we try to treat one, their stress level's so high that if we put them in a capture facility, we're probably causing more harm than doing good.

They're not domesticated at all. People think they're domesticated, but they're not domesticated. They become accustomed to what you're doing with them, but they still have that wild streak. That's why Cruella's still out there. We don't want to erase that wild streak.

PASSION

"It's great to be involved in something that is so critical to everyday life, to everybody—and to be in a state that is bountiful with resources."

JEFF SIMMONS

LALI HESS
THE JUNIPER SPOON

Lali Hess and her husband, Doug Miller, have lived on their five-acre homestead farm in Montgomery County since 2004. This is the bucolic base for Lali's catering business, The Juniper Spoon. Within sight of rows of blackberry bushes and fruit trees is Lali's kitchen, a gleaming state-of-the art workspace. When Lali and Doug decided to move from their home in Lancaster, Pennsylvania, they first considered settling in such foodie capitals as Madison, Wisconsin, Ann Arbor, Michigan, or Iowa City. "We looked at all of them and then we decided together that we wanted to be part of the revolution and not just bask in what had already been established," says Hess. "We were young and healthy and strong and had a little base of knowledge of agriculture—let's go to where we would do more."

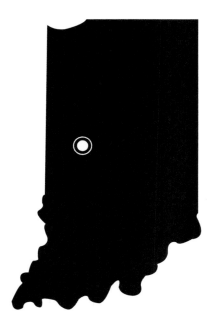

{Crawfordsville}

Part of the revolution

I grew up in a Mennonite family in Goshen. It was not traditional Mennonite. My dad is a professor, so it was more progressive, but there were certain traditions that were important to them that were brought from their farming background in Pennsylvania.

My dad gardened—we had an organic garden in our backyard, a compost pile, all of that—and this was in the seventies.

My mom made everything from scratch. I didn't even know there were canned soups until I left home.

They were influenced by a lot of the service work that happened through Goshen College and our church. They traveled overseas a lot, and so Mom made curry and baba ghanoush—she could make anything—and I had the stool up at the counter to watch her.

But what led me to want to cook as a profession is a little different. There are plenty of people who grow up with a good cook and a gardener as parents and don't end up cooking as a profession. For my college graduation, I asked my parents

to send me to a ten-day permaculture conference.

Permaculture is a philosophy of life and agriculture in which every resource is used to its fullest ability. It marries sustainability of household and garden with animal husbandry. It can be backyard gardening or it can be an agricultural system, but everything works together.

When my parents sent me to the permaculture conference it was like, "Oh, yeah, this is it. I'm not going to go to another country and change the world there." I

"What I'm trying to do is seduce people with good food."

realized that I was going to stay right here and grow my own food.

It took a few years to earn enough money, waiting tables, for me to be able to do what I wanted to do. So I took an internship first, and then I got my own farm, far away from anything. I felt starved for culture and for connection with people. There was no one like-minded there; it was just cheap land.

I drove to the Broad Ripple farmers' markets—this was in the late nineties—and I loved what I did. I had this beautiful farm and two acres of loved produce that I would take to market and make this beautiful display, but it wasn't sustainable for me.

Meanwhile, my customers were saying, "Well, what do you do with Asian eggplant? And what do you do with fennel bulb? What would you do with baby beets?" I didn't make any money, so all I did was cook with leftover vegetables. So I had five years of cooking vegetables in every possible form. Amazing vegetables: organic, beautiful, wonderful varieties.

Then a friend, who's an artist, had a gallery opening in Cincinnati and said, "They're just going to serve cheese and crackers and there's a $500 budget." This was more money than we could imagine at the time. It was at the Aronoff Center for the Arts, and my best friend and I said, "Sure! We'll make the food."

We outdid ourselves. The Aronoff asked if they could sign us up for a contract. We had some business cards made, and people started calling us. After the second year, we realized we were making more money catering than we were at the farmers' market.

At that point I met my husband. He had a house outside of Philadelphia in Lancaster County. I moved there with him, and we were there for two years. I worked for two caterers, and I wrote down everything. I knew nothing about business, but I learned how to be a caterer. Then we moved back to Indiana and went to start The Juniper Spoon.

We just knew what we were going to do. We were going to have a garden, an orchard, and try to supply as many vegetables as we could. We would also try to support local economy by getting vegetables and meats and cheeses around here.

Within ten miles of my house, I get pork, beef, lamb, chickens (I could get ducks if I wanted to), eggs, goat cheese, any vegetable I want, herbs. And we just picked a spot on the map and moved here; we didn't move here for those reasons. We were looking for a three-bedroom house on five acres anywhere around Indianapolis; I would guess this can probably be replicated all over the state.

There are cottage industries cropping up, and not all of these places were here when we moved here. The goat cheese place is new, the lamb place is new, where I get my vegetables is new. We can have anything.

But along with that, you need to have a consumer that is willing to go either out of their way to find things or willing to pay to have it provided to them conveniently. In Europe and certain coastal cities, they have created those networks. Here, we're having to create them from scratch. Our roads and our cities aren't designed to support cottage industry, but I hope there's a day when consumers and producers can work seamlessly together. I'm a consumer, but I also feed a lot of people because I do large events, so I'm trying to do that now, in a way. What I'm trying to do is seduce people with good food.

JEFF HAWKINS

HAWKINS FAMILY FARM, HOPE CSA

Jeff Hawkins didn't set out to be a farmer. A Lutheran pastor, he moved to his grandparents' farm in North Manchester in 1988 after coming to serve a local congregation the year before. Since then he has divided his time between church, his family farm, and nonprofit work with HOPE CSA, a program of hands-on pastoral education using Clergy Sustaining Agriculture aligned with the Samaritan Counseling Center in South Bend, where he is the clergy and congregation care director. "I live in a lot of different worlds," Hawkins says. Yet, for him, the farm provides a kind of metaphor that brings those worlds together.

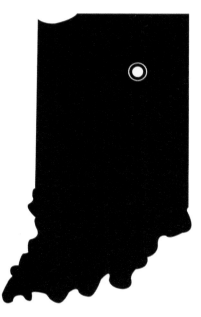

{ *North Manchester* }

Farming and churching

I did a lot of crazy things just using my imagination—maybe this would work, maybe that—and my neighbors would watch in the wonderful, understated way of country folk and say to me, you know, we tried sunflowers once—pause. What that pause meant was we experimented; it didn't work.

You know country people watch each other; farmers watch each other like crazy—so they'd been watching and, well, maybe some of what Jeff is doing makes a little sense. At least there was a little credibility rather than this crazy kid

who moved back to the farm and is trying some things.

I rented about sixteen acres up here from my dad and turned it into grass. They thought that was crazy. It's cropland, good cropland, and you don't turn that into pasture.

I observed the children and knew that as they grew older it would be a lot more difficult to have good conversations with them as they entered their teen years. It's not like we're going to sit down and have fifteen minutes of heart-to-heart quality talk—yeah, right Dad!

But what I learned was that if I said to them, "Hey, we're raising chickens, people like them, and if you kids would like to earn a little money, if you want to buy that first car, for example, you can earn it," they would trust me enough to say, "Well, okay."

So my son did morning chores, and my daughter did evening chores with me. We did the chickens, and what I learned was that, as we worked together, a lot of times they would just start talking and, if I was smart, I would not. There was just something about laboring together that

"*I observed that what I was doing on the farm was identical to what I was doing in the congregation in town.*"

accessed a different place, a freedom, a wider space, *a permission.* And there was something about the outer landscape and the inner landscape, the outdoors and the interior, that connected in ways that made a different quality of conversation.

As I was doing this, my bedtime reading was *Stockman Grass Farmer,* this kind of stuff nobody would read. But I was passionate about it, really asking the question: What's sustainable? What works in terms of a true ecological kind of agriculture?

What I observed was that what I was doing, compared to my neighbors who were all commercial production farmers, was totally flipped on its head. It appeared to me that the goal of commercial farming (you can call it production agriculture) was to, at all costs, really maximize production: more yield, more pounds, more efficiency. In order to do that, you would have to take what you could get in terms of health.

I had flipped that on its head. My main goal was health. I had to keep things healthy, but then I would have to take what I could get in terms of production.

I observed that what I was doing on the farm was identical to what I was doing in the congregation in town; that my neighbors, at that time, were all into the church growth thing, which is really maximizing production—more dollars, more square feet, even more faith, more disciples—noble kinds of things. But it was about production. And then it looked like they were taking what they could get in terms of health. So pastors were burning out, and congregations were in conflict.

In my congregation, I was not as concerned about production— we need more members, more dollars, more programs—I was more interested in qualitative kinds of things: health issues, so to speak, maturity in faith, and that kind of growth.

My farming and my churching went hand-in-hand in a lot of ways. When we moved here in 1988, some of what was on my mind was not only, oh, boy, I get to live on a farm, I like to raise things, I like to work with the earth, I like to work with animals, I like to work with my hands—but there was a theological or faith issue for me and it was: My goodness, I have this here; how am I supposed to use it? Is there a grander purpose behind this?

Some of where that question ended up taking me was [this]: If I was doing sustainable or ecological agriculture in order to learn how to church, perhaps other clergy ought to also. In other words, maybe there was a question here that we ought to be wrestling with in the church at large. And have we, in the church, sold out to an industrial paradigm?

In 2003, I left my congregation (I'd been there 16 years) and started a nonprofit organization called HOPE CSA. It wasn't to be traditional community supported agriculture; it was Hands-On Pastoral Education, using Clergy-Sustaining Agriculture [HOPE CSA]. I wanted to find a way that clergy could be here, be part of some of this—not a simulation—but really be part of this whole food thing, certainly part of the paradigm that I thought was more appropriate.

What we developed at that time was what we called a full-harvest share. Part of that had to do with my understanding of what health is on a farm; that there can't be one enterprise. It is not a monoculture; it has to be polyculture, many things supporting. There need to be animals, there need to be vegetables, there need to be all of this for health, and the farm needs to be its own economy, as much as possible. One thing feeding another. Production and consumption and return happening right here, on this ninety-nine acres.

JESÚS ALVAREZ

LYNETHE'S DELI AND PIEROGIES

"The Region" in northwest Indiana is well known for its ethnic diversity. In the early twentieth century, people from around the world and especially eastern Europe migrated here to work in the steel mills and at the enormous oil refinery in Whiting on the Lake Michigan coast. So it's probably not entirely surprising that a Mexican chef, Jesús Alvarez, has been dubbed by the Chicago Tribune *as Whiting's Pierogi King. Pierogi is a Polish word for an Eastern European delicacy, a dumpling made from unleavened dough that is first boiled or fried, then baked in butter with onions, and stuffed with an assortment of different fillings, from potatoes to prunes. Alvarez offers ten different types of pierogies at Lynethe's Deli and Pierogies, named for his wife (pictured here). We spent a summer morning with Alvarez and watched him serve a cavalcade of local old-timers and newcomers alike. We didn't see a soul leave the place who wasn't smiling.*

{*Whiting*}

The secret to pierogies

Most people from around here know about quality. If you change the recipes, they know. So people here know the right place to buy salads or food: They go with the little Mexican!

When you like food, it doesn't matter where it comes from. You can't get over the Italian food when I make it. In my house, for my boys, I make the best lasagna, with my own dough.

I started cooking in 1993. In the beginning I was a dishwasher. But after six months, I went to the office, I speak with the manager, very nice guy. I say, "I'm tired of washing dishes. If you don't train me right now to do something else, I quit!" I told him I wanted to try to learn how to make pies. So I start to learn how to make dough, and, after that, they started teaching me how to make the fillings.

Believe it or not, at that company, in a day, we make 5,000 pierogies. In a year, I learned how they do things there. They trained me for preparation in the kitchen.

I know how to make any kind of dough. With dumplings, they don't come with oil in the dough. The pierogies, they come with oil. That's the only thing you change. That's why they're soft. The filling can be anything. Somebody came in one day and

"If you know how to make good dough, everything is yours. It's in your hands."

asked me, "What's the secret to pierogies?" I say the only secret in pierogies is if you know how to make good dough. Everything else is no secret. If you know how to make good dough, everything is yours. It's in your hands.

You can put whatever you want in a pierogi. If you like rocks, you can put rocks in. That's true!

I have a customer, he's got a pizzeria in downtown Chicago. He comes with his whole family every Thursday for the ribs. And he tell me, "Jesús, you know how many places in downtown Chicago sell ribs? You don't have any idea! A thousand places sell ribs. But your ribs are the best! They don't compare, your ribs, with nobody. With nobody. I don't know how you do it, but your ribs are the best."

The secret's in the sauce. But you know every day we got something different. Yesterday it was the ribs and ham. Today is fish, shrimp. Tomorrow we got dumplings, stuffed cabbage. That's why people like to come here.

I name this place Lynethe's. The reason is because when I first met my wife, I ask her, "What's your name?" She tell me, "Lynethe."

I never heard that name before in my life! Well, she was around with me for three weeks. And every day I ask, "Excuse me, what's your name?" Every day I ask.

One day she tells me, "If you ask for my name one more time, you are a dead man."

So I made the name of the business Lynethe's, so I don't forget my wife's name! It's funny, but it's true. It's the real truth.

BARBARA SHA COX

INDIANA CAFO WATCH

Barbara Sha Cox and her husband, Dan, park their beloved Ford F-150 pickup truck at a Pizza Hut in Winchester, where the accommodating staff are in the habit of making a separate dining room available for special meetings. A retired nurse and third-generation farm woman, Barbara is the driving force behind indianacafowatch.com, a website dedicated to opposing the proliferation of corporate Concentrated Animal Feeding Operations (CAFOs) in Indiana. Barbara is a homegrown activist, a person who never fancied herself participating in a protest rally, let alone testifying before the state legislature. But over the course of the past decade, that's what she's done—speaking out for traditional farming lifestyles and Indiana's rural landscape.

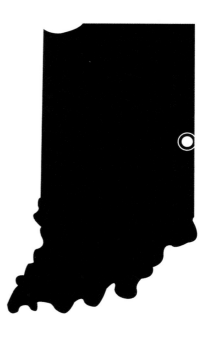

{ *Winchester* }

Voting with their forks

I grew up around a dairy farm. A hundred cows, very nice Guernsey operation. We rotated the crops, we rotated the alfalfa, the cows did their part: They were out in the corn, everything was fertilized, and it was all self-contained. Cows have the most wonderful personality, they really do. They are so personal. There's this whole connection between humans and animals if you just let it happen.

I went to nurses' training and my husband went to Korea. When he got back and I graduated, we were married and he started in banking. We first lived here, in Winchester, and his position took us to Anderson, Indiana. Mom and Dad kept the farm and we came back; our son spent his summers here.

Our parents aged, and we moved back to Richmond. At that point, Dad was in his eighties, and Mom had Alzheimer's, so we got involved. Mom was in a nursing home and Dad passed away in '88. The decision was to keep the farm or sell it. I could not sell it; it's third generation. I love it.

How much I love it is I had an old rider mower and I was mowing five to six acres. But I was paying about $6,000 a month for the nursing home for five years, and it was beginning to weigh on our cash reserves. When the mower broke, I hired a boy, and he and I push-mowed those barn lots for one summer because I said,

"People want to make this a blue or red issue; it's not."

"I don't have the money for a rider, but I am not going to let this farm go, and I am not going to let it go downhill." I knew if I was willing to get up every morning and go push that darn lawn mower every day, then I needed the farm.

One day a farmer came down the road. In a small community like this, the pickup truck's the best network we have to see each other on the back roads. He said, "You need to sign this petition against this huge dairy." I hadn't been involved in this, and I said, "Why would I want to sign a petition against a dairy?" I mean, that was all I knew was cows.

I started asking questions about the environment, about public health, about property rights, the whole ballpark of issues.

Now there're people in sixty-six counties that have joined our little network. I went to Best Buy and bought a computer. I told them I don't even know what to do with this thing, so why don't you just have it ready so when I go home and put in the password, I'm ready to email. By golly, they did! I told them my cause, and they really helped me.

Industrial agricultural associations and supporters have the money. The average rural citizen does not have that money or the knowledge. I got a new van in 2009; it now has 94,000 miles on it, and most of them are from meeting with people or running back and forth to the State House testifying, trying to get this information to people.

You have 55,000 hogs and 1,700 cows as your neighbors, plus all the poultry manure coming over from Ohio. You can imagine what it's like out there, especially if they're spreading manure. It's horrible.

So you've got property devaluation, got a lot of health issues, and I think one of the biggest things is your quality of life.

I realize that some producers do a very good job and are respectful of their neighbors. However, I continue to question why the good producers and their associations defend the bad actors. It seems to me that by having higher standards and not making excuses for the bad actors that would be a first step in protecting both the health of the citizens and the environment.

People want to make this a blue or red issue; it's not. We've had people from the very far left and the very far right join hands in this. I don't think it's wishful thinking, but what I'm seeing is the more education that's out there, the more people are voting with their forks, three times a day.

DAVID ROBB

HARVESTLAND FARM

Long before food was cool, David Robb was a pioneer in central Indiana's food scene. Now he manages the farming operation for the Indiana behavioral health system known as Aspire. Harvestland Farm represents a collaboration between Aspire, the city of Anderson, and Anderson University. It is one of three social enterprises created by Aspire to provide employment opportunities for people with mental disabilities. David's charge is to make Harvestland a self-sustaining business.

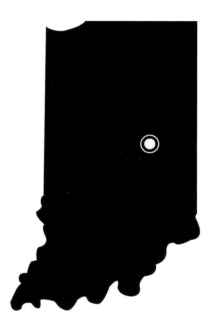

{Anderson}

It's a transformative experience

Aspire is a fairly large mental-health organization that provides a full range of different kinds of services, from people who just need walk-in counseling all the way up to people with long-term, severe mental illness who need twenty-four-hour care. We have group homes where people with long-term disabilities live. We also have caseworkers who help people with mental illness live independently. We have a homeless outreach program where we try and get people off the streets, into housing, and back into the workforce. We do HIV outreach.

Barb Scott was the main driver for this. She and our chief operating officer visited some organizations that blend farming with mental health services in the U.S. Barb wanted to do two things. She saw there was a great need to provide organically grown food to central Indiana communities, particularly around Anderson. Anderson is a pretty economically depressed area, and she felt there needed to be some good food produced locally.

The other initiative was to provide jobs for people with mental disabilities. The farm is called a social enterprise. The goal is to create employment and head towards being self-sustaining through our income source in order to pay our labor force.

Here on the farm, our staff is a fifty-fifty mix of people with disabilities and those without. So there's a lot of support here. There's a lot of understanding that if you get a little shaky, there might be a reason

"It creates a nice mix of different populations and a sense of normalcy."

for that other than the normal workplace reasons. We're always around to answer questions, to give support.

We grow year-round. We do farmers' markets; we also have our store. We do a CSA [community supported agriculture] every year, about a hundred-plus shares. Then we also do restaurants. We have eighteen acres here, and it's become a bit of a campus. It's very busy all the time. Buses come and go. It blends with the general public because people come to the store, my CSA members come, and it creates a nice mix of different populations and a sense of normalcy. I mean, if you've got mental illness, you could end up with people with mental illness and that's your whole life. But with what we do here, it's a real blend.

I guess my path started when I worked for the state of Indiana in economic development. I quit that job and opened a small deli-grocery in the Indianapolis City Market. I used to buy from a lot of farmers who were at the farmers' market. That introduced me to a lot of the people there.

I also was one of the originators of Slow Food Indy, back when it first formed. Then I was recruited by Traders Point Creamery to be their business development manager. I worked for them

for three to four years and helped to develop their business.

Barb Scott asked me to develop a business plan to where they could make this pay for itself. You get your best dollar from local vegetables off-season, not in July, August. Everybody's got what's in July and August: tomatoes, eggplant, peppers. But not everybody has lettuce and greens and arugulas and bok choys all winter, which we do.

I think our prospects are very good because we grow such a variety of product. There are things where people say, "What is that?" And we'll say, "Well, taste it." Some never will. But others will try different things. It creates a great reconnection with food and where it comes from.

And it's a transformative experience, too, because people here can plant seeds in a tray. Then they can transplant it. Three, four months later, they harvest it. In between, they've hoed it or done different things with it. Then they see it go out the door or take it home.

Farming is about patience and time. Nothing happens quickly. It's a different way to look at a busy electronic life. You can't hurry it up. You can't.

DON VILLWOCK

INDIANA FARM BUREAU

When we met, Don Villwock had served as the elected president of the Indiana Farm Bureau for ten years. The state's largest farm lobbying organization, Indiana Farm Bureau's mission is "to be an effective advocate for farmers and through its policies and programs, promote agriculture and improve the economic and social welfare of member families." Villwock and his wife, Joyce, became involved with Farm Bureau in 1979. "For the most part," he says, "I'm a corn, soybeans, wheat farmer that grew the operations with my wife's assistance and financing. She was a schoolteacher. So she put food on the table and paid our bills. Everything I made helped pay for the farm." Today, the Villwocks farm 4,000 acres in southwest Indiana.

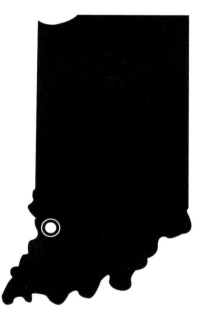

{*Edwardsport*}

What a great occupation

We are a farm organization that was started in 1919 to deal with the government about property taxes, which we thought were unfair. Bare property doesn't send kids to school. It doesn't require fire protection. It doesn't require police protection. But farmers in rural Indiana were paying for schools, and we just didn't think that was fair.

A lot of people know the name Farm Bureau because of the insurance company. Farmers couldn't get insurance during the Depression, so that's why we started our own insurance company. There's a Farm Bureau insurance company, or a relationship with an insurance company, in all fifty states.

It's ag communication and promotion, which we spend a lot of time and dollars to do. That's really our main function.

The rural/urban interface is our biggest challenge. A lot of people's dream is to buy a home and move out to the country. I understand that well. This old farm boy couldn't live in town. I don't like close neighbors. I've been spoiled, or at least I think I have.

"What a great occupation to be in—you get to be outside, you get to be with Mother Nature."

Most people in Indiana want to have a big yard and a view and a greenscape, but they don't realize they're moving into an area where a combine only goes twenty miles an hour and takes up eighteen feet on a twenty-foot wide road. Meanwhile, they're trying to get to work and they're late and they can't pass. And because the road's so narrow, the combine can't get over to let them around. So we get these wave gestures; sometimes not all fingers are present.

There are sights and smells of agriculture that have been omnipresent since the first cow or pig walked on the face of this earth. Some people don't like that and they want to shut us down and petition and take us to court. Farm Bureau passed a right-to-farm law that said if you're there first, you've always been a farm, you've maintained it as a farm, you can still run it as a farm.

But in northern Hamilton County and Fishers and Westfield and Carmel, as people move into ag areas, we have a lot of issues.

And so it's hard for a farmer whose grandpa started this farm. His dad was here. Now there's tremendous competition. The only way to bring a son or daughter back to the farm is to bring livestock there, because that gives an opportunity to diversify. It gives the farmer another profitable enterprise.

So then they build these hog units on the farm and, all of a sudden, we have a massive firestorm: a protest and hearings and actually threats. We've had up to twenty-two counties where there are ferocious hearings and name-calling and fighting and feuding going on.

They looked at the records and in 1950 the hog population in Harrison County was twenty times what it is today. Quite often those pigs were out in pasture, in a hog wallow that smelled 365 days out of the year.

Whereas these confinement operations, they go out and inject their manure according to a nutrient management plan and it smells for three days. The rest of the year, you don't even know they're there.

Our problem is people are disconnected from their food. They think it comes from Kroger. They think it comes from Marsh. Or they think it comes from the farmers' market. They don't realize in this equation that there's a farmer involved, that he takes risks, deals with the environment, deals with markets, deals with the government, and, hopefully, at the end of the day, he has a healthy, nutritious, affordable food product that he can sell to someone to put on the shelf.

It's a complex food system we live in. I don't think there's any farmer that intentionally distorts the food or does something wrong on purpose or takes a shortcut that may hurt food safety in some way. For the most part, farmers want to do good. They want to do the right thing. And what a great occupation to be in—you get to be outside, you get to be with Mother Nature. My best day on a farm is when I'm there in a field by myself.

SONNY BECK

BECK'S HYBRIDS

Sonny Beck has roots. He says he's only lived in two houses: the white frame house his grandfather Lawrence built (pictured here) in 1912, still standing adjacent to Beck's Atlanta, Indiana, headquarters and the house Sonny built for himself, a half-mile down the road. The Beck family has farmed in Hamilton County since 1901, when Lawrence Beck bought the eighty-acre farm that became the cornerstone for Beck's Hybrids, currently the largest, independent family-owned retail seed company in the United States. In 1937, Lawrence and Sonny's father, Francis, planted three acres each of hybrid parent seed corn they were offered by the Purdue University botany department. They used a two-row, horse-drawn planter and harvested the crop by hand. This would be the first crop known as Beck's Superior Hybrids. Sonny and his wife, Glendia, joined the family business in 1964.

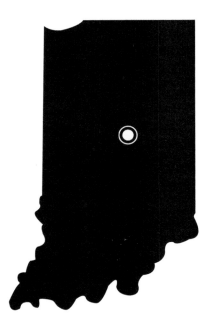

{ Atlanta }

Everything goes around comes around

I just want to learn something new all the time. So I started doing testing. Should you use more fertilizer or less? How about the new chemicals that are coming out for weed control?

I found out that other farmers wanted to know about these things, too. So we invited them in. They'd ask: "Will you test this?" Sure. We kept adding one more, two more tests every year of different things they wanted to know to help them farm. It's up to seventy tests that we have going now.

We kind of filled a void there. It's one of the big reasons for the growth of the company because we provide this information free to anybody. They don't even have to buy corn. After awhile people do come back and say, "I've been reading your information, getting value from it for years and I felt like I ought to come by and buy something." So everything goes around, comes around.

Anybody can run a test plot and see which corn yields the most or which soybean yields the most. That's what most of us in the seed business do. What's different about this company is that we also run tests to show what happens if it's not the best conditions out there. How do you

> *"Progress always means change, so I'm most encouraged by farmers that understand you have to have change."*

survive when the conditions aren't as good? Which hybrids and which practices should you use to get more yield if there aren't the perfect conditions? I think that's why our customers like to do business with us. That's what they tell us. We're not about just trying to extract an extra dollar from them to give to our shareholders.

We're privately owned. We're independent. We have the ability to run the company differently than a public company. Most of America is developed into public companies. There's nothing wrong with that model. But if I'm the CEO of a public company, who's my boss? It's really the next quarter. It's Wall Street. It's the investor that took his hard-earned money and put it in my company. So my first loyalty has to be to return him a larger return on investment than to somebody else or he takes his money and puts it in Coca Cola or General Motors.

Now as owners of a family-owned corporation like we are here— my three children, myself, and our spouses—we can run the company without always thinking about who do we have to pay up here. I can only wear one pair of shoes at a time, one pair of boots. After that, we're looking at how our customers can make more money; how to do more tests that wouldn't be economically feasible if I had to defend them against shareholders.

Progress always means change, so I'm most encouraged by farmers that understand you have to have change. The only truly sustainable, competitive advantage is the ability to learn and adapt faster than your competition. And farmers have to realize their competition, even though it's their neighbor, is other farmers. That's who they're competing with when they go to market. We can help them learn to farm better and make more yield, so we can help them compete against their neighbor. What we're about is helping them on the production side. It's up to them to figure out on the marketing side how to make more money.

If you study the weather records, even though all farmers complain about not enough rainfall in July and too much in April, we have a very uniform set of rainfall all year. So we don't need much irrigation here to grow good corn. We have a natural competitive advantage. We're not the first ones to realize this; people understood it many, many years ago. This is the Corn Belt.

JEFF SIMMONS

ELANCO

Jeff Simmons is president of Elanco, the animal health division of Eli Lilly and Company. Elanco's mission is to develop innovative, safe technologies to make healthier, more efficient production animals. "At Elanco, we talk about being in the people business," says Simmons. "Our vision is clear: food and companionship enriching life." The company is involved in efforts to help end childhood hunger in Indianapolis and is working to bring 100,000 developing-world families out of hunger through a partnership with Heifer International. Simmons's family continues to farm in upstate New York.

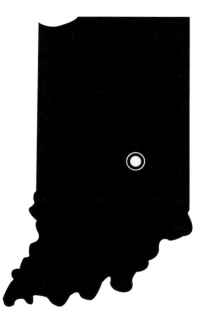

{Greenfield}

The hunger inside

I grew up on a farm, and I don't think that ever leaves you. I was in FFA [also known as Future Farmers of America], which taught me that while the essence of food is back on the farm, agriculture is actually bigger than the farm. It's also about the world. It's about providing something that is absolutely essential to people.

Life is complex; every individual has a different story. But there are two essentials everybody should have, two rights everybody should have when they're born. They need to have hope for the future, to dream. And they need food.

They need to be nourished, no matter where they are in the world.

Coming from a farm background into this company, and Elanco and Lilly being Indiana-based in the heart of farm country, as well as living in Brazil and Europe, and traveling all over the seventy-five countries Elanco's in, opened my eyes to the importance of innovation in agriculture.

A little flame became an inferno for me personally in April of 2000. I had been living in Brazil for four months and was learning that I was in a kind of bubble. I

lived in a private community and rode in a car with a driver. I was in this great country, but I didn't get to experience it other than with this one guy who worked the gate at my community. His name was Joaquin. He taught me Portuguese. I got to know him. He was my ten-minute exposure to the real life in Brazil at the beginning and end of every day.

One rainy night in April 2000 there was a knock on the door, and that knock changed my wife's and my life. I opened the door and there stood Joaquin, this broken man, tears coming off his nose.

> *"It's great to be involved in something that is so critical to everyday life, to everybody—and to be in a state that is bountiful with resources."*

Not the bright, exuberant Brazilian that I was used to. And his two daughters were standing next to him. Inside, there were my two daughters of similar age.

He exposed me to something I had never experienced. He told me our landlord—his employer—was having terrible financial problems. He hadn't been paid in a long time. "These are my daughters. I'm sorry, Mr. Jeff, that I'm here, but you're the only person I could come to."

They hadn't eaten in two days.

It shook me emotionally. And I've never lost that. His picture remains in my home office.

We live in a state, Indiana, that is productive, that has resources that can help feed the world. But more people today are living with food as an issue than those that are not. To me, there is an excitement here that this issue carries a moral responsibility bigger than an economic opportunity for Elanco. It's great to be involved in something that is so critical to everyday life, to everybody—and to be in a state that is bountiful with resources.

I travel around the world, and optimism probably doesn't reign as strongly as I see it here in Indiana. What makes me proud is the way people here see agricultural production as being linked to food and the social need to serve.

In the next forty years we are going to need 100 percent more food. Seventy percent of that has to come from technology. We can make it reality, but it's going to take products from companies like ours. It's going to take better practices on the farm that are going to be discovered at Purdue University. It's going to take

leaders that are going to come up with the next level of genetics.

The many hundreds of employees in Indiana that work for Elanco see this. We have a big cause. A lot of people expect a lot from us. We have less land than we've ever had. Water's an issue. We have to increase food production, and it must be done in an innovative way.

But to get innovation you have to have more than an idea. That idea has to be implemented in practice. A true innovation is something that works. In the case of genetics, you have to be able to figure out how to get an animal to perform on a different kind of feed or a different level of water. You have to be able to develop products and technologies that can produce more with less or handle diseases that are emerging or haven't been seen yet.

These are all aspects of what the World Health Organization defines as the 70 percent solution, or 70 percent of the answer to making food more affordable, safe, and abundant.

We ask our employees to take half a day each quarter, on Elanco's time, to go, take their family, and experience a hungry face. You have to see a face that hasn't been fed in a day. Or try fasting for thirty hours and feel like a lot of young kids in Africa that don't eat. I think that's important. Once that happens, the vision, the understanding of the need to increase food production—it becomes more of a personal cause. And I think Indiana has a lot of cause-centered leaders that are agriculturally based, that see this as a great opportunity.

The hunger that's greater is the hunger inside of us to become part of something bigger. People want to become part of something bigger than themselves.

ARTISANAL

"If you do it good enough, long enough, they will come."

JUDY SCHAD

JUDY SCHAD
CAPRIOLE FARMSTEAD GOAT CHEESE

The goats scamper up to greet you at Judy Schad's Capriole Farmstead. Located in New Albany, a stone's throw from the Ohio River, Capriole has been winning first place awards for over twenty years, including gold medals for its Mont St. Francis, Sofia, and Old Kentucky Tomme cheeses at an international competition in Basilicata, Italy. In addition to its fresh goat cheese, Capriole also produces surface ripened, aged, and specialty cheeses. "I feel like it takes ten years to really get cheese where you want it," says Judy. "We are still working on things that we started fifteen or twenty years ago."

{ *New Albany* }

What goat milk is for

In some ways, in our part of the state, I don't feel like I'm from Indiana. We're so close to Kentucky, Louisville's always been my big hometown. We get Louisville news, we get Louisville food, so our food culture here is a little more upper south. I grew up on persimmon pudding. It's all Ohio River Valley.

I had a wonderful grandmother who was an incredible cook and cooked out of her garden. You know, the pigs and chickens ate what wasn't good enough for the table. Everything was fresh. My mother was a great cook. I got *The Joy of Cooking* when I was fourteen and was making puff pastry by the time I was sixteen.

My involvement with cheeses started with the goats. We came to the country as really stupid city people. We knew nothing; we had one fiasco after another: the acre of asparagus that all got drowned because we didn't have enough dirt to put in the trenches ... It was just one thing after another.

I came here with the idea of growing my own food and having our own milk. I wanted a cow. But we had a neighbor who said, "Oh, you don't want a cow. You don't want to get up at five o'clock in the morning and go over there when it's twenty below zero and have to clean all the shit off the back of the cow before you can milk her. You don't want to do that. You need a goat." That was how it all started.

Goats are probably the city person's idea of what an animal should be. They're about half cow, half dog: smart, clever, interesting, different personalities, friendly. If you feed a baby on a bottle, they're going to know you three years later. When you walk in a barn and animals come up and nibble on you, you know that somebody's taken good care of them. They don't run when you come in. They're very, very personable, and we just fell in love with them.

About 1982, we took the goats to the Indiana State Fair and got Best of Show, had a great time—the kids did, fooling around with them—but we had all this milk. By that time there were fifteen goats, and what are you going to do with all of it? The kids didn't want to drink it because they were city kids who grew up on 2 percent and you couldn't disguise it or do anything to it. I'd put it in half-gallon milk containers but no, that is goat milk—they knew!

About that time, I ate my first goat cheese from Lettie Kilmoyer. It was on the menus in Louisville and in retail stores. You could buy the little white tubes of what everybody thinks of as goat cheese, even though there are 250 different kinds, they think of the white stuff: That's goat cheese. And I was just, oh, oh, my god, this is unbelievable. This is what goat milk is for.

When you think about it, in every country where they have it, that is what goat milk is for. Children may drink it in the home but, by and large, it's not marketed as milk. It's marketed as cheese. And that's the Mediterranean thing: Cow milk is for drinking; goat milk is for cheese.

I thought, well, this is incredible. I started making it in the kitchen and bought this little book called *Cheesemaking Made Easy* (I still have it here somewhere) from Ricki Carroll up at New England Cheesemaking Supply and, after three years of this, I said, "We need to think about selling this. Let's turn another dream into a nightmare and do the goat cheese thing."

In a fresh goat cheese I look, first of all, for that clean, lemony acidity. But what I think makes ours different is texture. This cheese is all hand-ladled very carefully—300-gallon vats into baskets and into molds so as not to disturb that texture. If it's a more industrial cheese, likely it's been pumped with a low velocity pump that breaks down that textural thing. So ours is really light. We still do it the old way.

It's real laborious. It takes probably two to three hours in the morning to dip that vat of cheese and to ladle it, and then it drains. And about six hours into the drainage, once the curd has settled and formed, we salt it and hang it. The next day we come back and package it. That's the basic fresh white stuff that we all think of as *chevre*.

My market did not begin locally. It had to be regional and even national because there wasn't that much awareness of goat cheese. But the great thing about that was that our entrée was through chefs, so there was immediate validity for an unusual product because it started in the restaurants. In the 1970s, there was goat cheese on the East and West Coasts, but it was not the norm here. It was a bunch of crazy women with a handful of goats who really started the whole thing.

My best friend is Mary Keehn from Cypress Grove in Humboldt County, California—she makes a cheese called Humboldt Fog—and Paula Lambert from the Mozzarella Company. In a way, my community has been this cohort of fellow women, primarily cheese makers, from Massachusetts to Texas to California to Oregon. We all still know each other. It's still a very small world. We haven't begun to die off quite yet, so my theory is, if you do it good enough, long enough, they will come. And that's what we've tried to do.

TIM BURTON

BURTON'S MAPLEWOOD FARM

Follow a serpentine road through the heart of a maple forest to Medora and you'll find yourself at Tim and Angie Burton's Maplewood Farm, site of the annual National Maple Syrup Festival, held on the first and second weekends in March. In addition to the festival, the Burtons produce a line of gourmet maple syrups, including varieties with flavors infused by rum and bourbon. Burton's syrups have been adopted by a who's who of Chicago chefs, including Paul Kahan of Blackbird, Avec, and the Publican; Rick Bayless of Topolobampo and Frontera Grill; Art Smith of Table Fifty-Two; Ina Pinkney of Ina's; and the Ritz Carlton's Mark Payne, who also uses Burton's products for room service.

{ *Medora* }

No better place

Angie and I owned a systems integration business, where we dealt in technology and that type of thing. We had a young man, Joe Evans, that worked for us as a laser technician, and, in January and February, he would ask if he could knock off a little early during the day. I said, "Well, sure, as long as you have your bases covered."

Well, then one request turned into two, two turned into three, and by the fourth time around I said, "Joe, it's none of my business, but why are you knocking off so early? What are you doing?" And he said, "Oh, man, I'm helping the Miller family collect sap to make maple syrup. It's a lot of fun; you should go with me."

So I did.

I went over to the Miller's farm. There was a whole army of Miller kids and nephews and nieces converged there that evening. And they all had their four-wheelers and small trailers with the small tanks.

We went with our five-gallon buckets from tree to tree, emptying out the sap. Then we'd transfer that into the larger tanks that the tractors or the four-wheelers would pull.

And I got it. I got the whole excitement thing. What impressed me was the lost social aspect of doing this, everybody coming together. And it wasn't just the family; it was neighbors and friends.

We're surrounded by maple trees, so we

> *"There's no better place for a National Maple Syrup Festival than Indiana because this is where the season starts."*

decided we'll just do this ourselves. We started tapping our own trees, using conventional buckets. It's more labor intense, but we do it because it's what people enjoy seeing. It's going back to the lost social aspect.

There were a couple of things that triggered us to look at taking our product beyond the local farmers' market. I have a friend by the name of Scott Hutcheson, also known as the "Hungry Hoosier," from Lebanon, Indiana. Scott was telling me about this farmer from northern Indiana by the name of Greg Gunthorp, who decided to call a pretty well-known restaurant in Chicago called Charlie Trotter's. Of course, that got my mind going. I thought, well, gosh, if Greg can do that, why can't another farmer-producer do that? I'm not bashful.

About that same time, I saw Judy Schad from Capriole Cheese. We were having lunch at Goose the Market in Indy and she said, and I quote, "You need to get your ass up to Chicago because it's happening there." And I said, "What's happening?" She said, "The food scene. The chefs up there are starving for locally sourced product."

So I'm thinking: Okay, Scott said this, Judy's saying this. I need to check into it. I phoned Green City Market in Chicago, and they said their application deadline had passed, but they didn't have a maple syrup producer, which really surprised me. No one from northwest Indiana, no one from Michigan, no one from Wisconsin was going to that market.

So we got in there. Two months we were going up every Wednesday and every Saturday. It's about five hours from here, one-way.

That first Saturday, this guy comes riding up on a ten-speed bike. We had no idea what to expect when you're dealing with a chef.

What is a chef going to look like? To me, a chef looks like Chef Boyardee. Well, this really cool-looking cat rides up and he goes, "Hi, I'm Paul Kahan. I'm a chef here in town, and I heard you guys were going to be here and I'm really—I think the word he used was 'stoked'—that you're here."

That was our first interaction with a Chicago chef. I was like, Whoa! That's a Chicago chef? Then we just started meeting more chefs and introducing ourselves to different restaurants.

At about the same time, Angie and I came up with the idea of starting a maple syrup festival. Our family has always been supportive of Riley Hospital for Children's Cleft and Craniofacial Anomalies program. Our niece, Katelyn, was born with a unilateral cleft lip and palate, and our sister and brother-in-law wanted to give something back to Riley. So we started the Heads Up!!! Foundation, and all the proceeds from the festival could go there to help Riley's Camp About Face.

We Googled National Maple Syrup Festival and would you believe it? There's no National Maple Syrup Festival. Unreal! So I immediately trademarked it, and now we have the trademark to the National Maple Syrup Festival—and it's here in Indiana.

When we mention this to people, they have the same reaction: It's not in Vermont? But what's interesting is that there's no better place for a National Maple Syrup Festival than Indiana because this is where the season starts. Indiana is on the southwestern fringe of the Maple Belt. This is where the first maple syrup is produced in the world. Not just in the United States—in the world. Most people don't know that.

This is the oldest agricultural crop in Indiana. Actually, maple syrup was being produced by the Native Americans. So there's no better place to be.

CHRIS ELEY

GOOSE THE MARKET, SMOKING GOOSE

At Goose the Market, Chris and Mollie Eley's brainchild in the Fall Creek Place neighborhood of Indianapolis, an enthusiasm for new culinary experiences is paired with the time-honored art of charcuterie. Chris is an Indianapolis native, with a wide-ranging pedigree including culinary school in Providence, Rhode Island; Purdue's hotel/restaurant program; and stints with Chicago's legendary Lettuce Entertain You Enterprises, as well as the White Restaurant Group, where he worked as an executive chef and troubleshooter. Since moving from Chicago, Chris and Mollie have opened the original Goose the Market and Smoking Goose, a smoking/cure house designed to supply local restaurants.

{Indianapolis}

From the source

I think I've always just loved meat. I like everything about appreciating an animal for what it's worth, appreciating its life, and appreciating everything you can do with it. I don't think it was any one certain thing that turned me on to meat, but more a process starting originally with cutting steaks (probably the simplest thing you can do) and then asking where does this steak come from, how is it cut, what makes it more flavorful or less

flavorful, more tender or less tender. In that process of learning more and more about the animal, I enjoyed doing more with meat and preservation.

Charcuterie is the art of preserving meat. It includes smoking and curing and different techniques. It evolved during the prerefrigeration days, when meat had to be stored and kept by other means. Portions of the animal that couldn't be eaten immediately had to be preserved

through salt curing, through fermentation. It was done with very little in the way of chemicals, very few additives. Salt played a huge role, as well as sealing things with rendered fat. These created flavors that I think we've grown accustomed to loving in our diets, and creating these flavors has become more of an art than a preservation technique now that we have refrigeration.

It starts with butchering. I started learning

"You learn by cutting yourself. You can only do it so many times before you realize that you need to either quit doing it or practice getting better."

butchering techniques in culinary school. The basics: You get to see and kind of experience it in culinary school, but you don't really learn it until you do it day-in, day-out—and that was done mostly in restaurants, hotels, and country clubs over a number of years, working in different kitchens, being able to do different things. Once you learn the butchering aspect, how to break down animals and utilize them fully, then you start to pick up on different things in terms of charcuterie.

You learn by cutting yourself. You can only do it so many times before you realize that you need to either quit doing it or practice getting better. Knife skills and butchering are very different. In a typical professional kitchen, there's a lot of slicing, chopping, small knife work. What we do is seam butchering, which is essentially carving out each individual muscle rather than cutting directly through muscle. It's a different style because of the delicate knife: more tip work, less chopping, less slicing. It's more surgeon-like in terms of accuracy; we're dismantling and taking apart an animal, saving and not damaging the muscles. It's a matter of practicing.

The biggest thing that attracted me to Indianapolis is that I grew up here; I had roots here. That's always important when starting a business, a strong foundation. You need a lot of support. I hadn't lived here in five or six years, but the other thing that really attracted me to Indianapolis was that it had a lot of potential. It was the city where I felt we could make the greatest impact. If we opened in Chicago, it would have been challenging with all the competition; property is extremely expensive and so is labor.

What we faced here was doing something that no one else was doing, going out on a limb. We had to see if people would gravitate toward what we did or whether it would be too foreign and wasn't something the city needed.

But people are becoming more involved and more aware of their food. Not just where it comes from but how it's raised, how it's produced, who's handling it. Even the government is taking a more hands-on approach with the FDA plan to track food from its origins to the table. This is quite easy for us, since we deal with very few producers compared to larger commodity food markets. We have had an advantage because we've been doing it from the source, knowing where everything comes from. We visit these places, we spend time there, and the people that raise the animals spend time here.

We really don't do any advertising, so the only way you can grow is through word-of-mouth. It comes down to doing the best that you can every day and focusing on how we can get better, how we can improve what we're doing. I've always believed that if you're not getting better, you're getting worse. You can't stay the same.

I think that mentality has helped us in a small market. Every time you come to the shop, there's something new and something different. If you come into a 2,000-square-foot shop—say we want you to come in once a week—it's going to get very monotonous if we're not constantly offering new things and doing things you can't find other places. I think our word-of-mouth was built on the fact that we were willing to do whatever it took to really try and do the best we possibly could.

GREG GUNTHORP
GUNTHORP FARMS

If there's such thing as a celebrity farmer, Greg Gunthorp might make the grade. From his family farm in LaGrange, Greg has become the go-to guy for some of the world's most well-known chefs by selling his pork and poultry to such restaurants as Charlie Trotter's, named "The Best Restaurant in the World for Wine and Food" by Wine Spectator *magazine. Gunthorp's commitment to raising animals in a sustainable, healthy way is reflected by a sticker on the door to the USDA-approved processing facility he's managed to set up on his property: "These pigs don't do drugs—just grass."*

{ *LaGrange* }

I'm a pig farmer at heart

Gunthorp Farms got started a long time ago. I'm at least a fourth-generation, pastured pig farmer. But in 1998, I actually sold pigs for less than what my grandpa sold them for in Great Depression—I got as low as four cents a pound for pigs. Really: for live pigs.

Up until that point, my family had always made a decent living raising pigs the same way we do now and selling them as live animals on the commodity market. Then I saw in magazines

and papers that it was kind of trendy for people to want free-range animals raised without all the chemicals.

That's what my family had always been doing. I thought, "This can't be that difficult."

Well, it was that difficult.

I've put in way too many hours. But we have a USDA-inspected slaughter and processing operation right here on the farm. We raise pigs, chickens, ducks,

turkeys—all on pasture. Process them here. Deliver them mostly to restaurant customers in Chicago, Indianapolis, and Detroit.

We developed a really good clientele mainly through word of mouth. I spent an awful lot of time in Chicago beating on doors and on the telephone, calling people. Then Steve Bonney, with Sustainable Earth in West Lafayette, had me speaking on the sustainable ag circuit. I was out in Columbia, Missouri, and when I was finished with my presentation, I was talking with a group of farmers in the back of the room, and one of them told me he had a friend in Oregon who had been shipping whole, dressed pigs to Chicago, but he was going to quit raising pigs. He said, "You ought to give that restaurant a call because I know they're looking for a pig farmer."

And I called them.

To this day I don't know why Matt Merges, the chef de cuisine at Charlie Trotter's, answered the phone. He doesn't normally do that, let alone talk to people. But he probably talked to me for fifteen, twenty minutes. He was extremely knowledgeable about pigs, asked an awful lot of good questions, like what breed we were raising, what we were feeding them, how we were getting them processed. He said, "Well, why don't you just bring us a pig next week?"

So we started selling to Charlie Trotter's in Chicago. The rest, I guess, is history.

The breed of pig makes a definite difference in the taste of the animal. We raise a heritage breed of pigs. All of our pigs are either full-blooded Durocs or 50 percent Durocs. The way they're fed makes a difference, too. We're not shooting for white, lean pork. Our pork still has some color to it. We're wanting it to be marbled, wanting it to have a good fat cover on it, so we're not feeding excessive amounts of protein.

We're letting our pigs develop slower, put a little more age on them. That gives them time to develop more flavor. They're raised outside their whole life, so they have variety in their diet. They're eating some grass or clover. When acorns fall from the trees, they're eating acorns and, in spring, they're eating some mulberries.

And they're delivered fresh to a very small plant, where they're processed by hand by skilled butchers.

We also raise chickens, ducks, and turkeys. We actually started raising our chickens and ducks for Rick Bayless at Frontera Grill. I tried my darndest to sell them pork, but they're extremely loyal to their farmers and they already had a pig farmer. But Tracey Vowell, who was the managing chef at the time, said, "We're really looking for somebody to raise our poultry."

We'd always raised a few chickens for our own consumption and for friends—150, 200 a year. I think we did 12,000 that first year with Frontera. It was a huge learning curve.

It's turned out to be a really rewarding experience. My family always sold live pigs on the commodity market, and now, as a farmer, I feel sorry for people growing stuff for the commodity market because they don't get the respect they deserve for the products they're producing. We sell to the best restaurants in the Midwest and possibly the world, and they just have the greatest appreciation for what we do. That makes everything we do so worthwhile. It's a night-and-day difference: growing products for a market versus growing them for people who actually appreciate what you're doing.

This is an exciting time. Local, sustainable agriculture in Indiana is growing by leaps and bounds. You know, I'm probably the very, very fortunate Gunthorp generation, being in the right place, at the right time because my family's been doing this forever, but now people actually appreciate it.

I'm a pig farmer at heart, always will be. We've raised an awful lot of birds, but I'm still a pig farmer at heart. When you see a sow with her litter of baby pigs walking behind her, you know the whole thing is worthwhile. It really is.

SHARON YODER

YODER POPCORN

Indiana is one of the nation's top popcorn producing states, and the Yoders have been selling popcorn up in northeast Indiana for generations. Although not Amish themselves, the Yoder's Topeka shop is located in a rural community where motor vehicles share the road with numerous horses and buggies. The Yoders sell a variety of popping corn, including Tiny Tender White, Red, Blue, and Sunburst, as well as a full line of salts, seasonings, and oils. Yoder Popcorn Shoppe has been featured in Gourmet Magazine. *One October morning, Sharon Yoder took the time to tell us what makes popcorn pop.*

{ *Topeka* }

Made to pop

Yoder Popcorn was started by my great uncle and great grandfather, both of them Yoders. That was in the late 1930s—1936, I've been told. What they did was mostly sell truckloads of popcorn they bought from local farmers. They usually left it on the ear, but they could also shell it and sell it in fifty-pound bags.

We lived on the farm and there was not a lot of money for frivolous snacks. In the evenings, when guests would come, we'd make a big dish pan of popcorn and serve it with grape juice or lemonade. I mean that was a treat.

There are actually three kinds of corn. There's the sweet corn that you eat in the summertime. Then there's field corn, which is used a lot for livestock feed and cornmeal. Popcorn is much, much harder. It's a different seed. It's made to pop.

They say that they have found corn in Indian caves from way, way back that still popped. Popcorn will last forever as long as you can retain the moisture in the kernel. That's what makes popcorn popcorn.

There's moisture in the kernel and when it gets hot enough, the steam inside it will make it explode and turn into a popcorn kernel. So long as you take good care of it and keep it in something tightly sealed, you can have popcorn for years. It doesn't go bad.

Different varieties will have different flavors and textures. Part of that is the seed. And the season—that's another thing. If it's dry and hot and you don't get the moisture at the right time, it can wreak havoc.

There're folks that like the big-kernel popcorn, like you get at ballparks and theaters. That's your least expensive corn because it's easiest to grow and it's yellow.

The Sunburst pops big, like the large yellow one does, but it's got some red markings on it. It tends not to have quite as much hull. The bigger your kernel, the more hull—that's the stuff that gets caught in your teeth.

If you get smaller kernels, as a rule, they have less hull. The Blue or the Red, they have a very crispy or crunchy kernel. They're a little bit harder. If you don't like a crunchy kernel, you don't want those.

I like crunchy kernels. I like crispy. So I like the Tiny Tender White. I also like the Red and the Blue for a change. I'm not much into the chewy, big yellow one. It's okay, but it's not my favorite.

In my opinion, oil makes the best popcorn. I do not care for hot air popcorn; it's too dry. I like our canola oil, because it has butter flavor added. Coconut oil is also very good, but it's high in saturated fat and that's not so good. Although now they're saying that coconut oil's got some good properties, so who knows? There are some people who use olive oil to pop their popcorn.

You just need a good quality oil because some oils, if they're not as pure, they can burn before your popcorn pops. Popcorn needs a fairly high heat in order to make it pop well. If people complain, we say, "Where'd you get your oil?"

We had a high school that used a big kettle for their ball games and they were ready to buy a new kettle, which is like $500 or $600, because they were burning their popcorn. That's the main part of your machine. But the guy at the place where we get our poppers said, "Ah, have them change their oil first."

They changed their oil to some that we carry—no problem.

TED HUBER

HUBER'S STARLIGHT DISTILLERY

The Hubers have been farming along the Ohio River since before the Civil War. Now the Huber's Orchard, Winery and Vineyards, with over 600 acres of gently rolling countryside, a large market, restaurant, and wine shop, provides a major southern Indiana agritourism destination. In 2000, Ted Huber helped write legislation to open Indiana for the production of craft spirits and artisan distilleries. When the bill passed in 2001, Huber's Starlight Distillery was ready to begin production.

Ten years later, Huber's received top honor awards for its distilled spirits during the American Distilling Institute's annual conference in Portland, Oregon. Huber's was the top winner in the overall brandy category. Other award winners included Huber's Grappa, Applejack, Apple Brandy, and Reserve Brandy.

{ *Starlight* }

True American spirits

This farm has been in my family since 1843 and the unique thing about it is growing up in a family-owned and -operated business, having all of the aunts and uncles and great aunts and uncles coming around, talking about all the stuff that happened years and years ago.

Something they always talked about was how we made this great brandy. Then Grandma and Grandpa led me through

it. So, at the age of fifteen, I started thinking about distilling.

One winter we had a very large apple crop and I decided to go ahead. I ran some apples off and we fermented some of that apple juice into wine and distilled it down. I was surprised at how good that stuff was. So I threw it in an old whiskey barrel, like Grandma said we used to always do, and made the old style

applejack out of that. Year after year, that stuff kept getting better and better.

Applejack is one of the true American spirits. That and bourbon. Those two are part of the American culture. Back years and years ago, applejack was actually used as currency in a lot of areas. You traded, or you did this job, for X amount of applejack.

People don't realize that southern Indiana

was the wine growing capital of the United States for many, many years. Where Napa Valley is today, southern Indiana was around 200 years ago. This is also where all the apples were being grown and where a lot of the applejacks were being made. Long before whiskey and bourbon were popular, applejack was really popular. If you look at some of the old drink recipes, you'll see that applejack was a base for a lot of those.

Our style of applejack had a slight bourbon edge to it since the bourbon capital is literally twenty-five to thirty minutes from here, in Louisville, Kentucky. We used the same cooperage and a lot of the same techniques that the distillers south of the river did. We used the exact same barrels that bourbon was aged in and it brought that same flavor.

I carried on the old family tradition, using those barrels, which is a unique flavor profile to this area of the United States. It's completely different than the applejacks of the East Coast that use more of a European style, a European toast level and style of barrel. We use the traditional fifty-gallon American white-oak charred barrel.

Even at ten years, wineries are typically small and still trying to get their groove. But distilleries are typically multigenerational before they get up and going and have enough backlog of aged products. We were very fortunate to hit the ground running. You have to

start with great fruit and that's what gives us the advantage.

Our apple brandies and our grape brandies are grown here on the farm. We're growing the fruits, we're crushing the fruit, making the raw product into wines, and then distilling those products. They're all aging on the property. We're doing the blends. Right now, as young as we are, we're doing multiple blends for multiple years. So we're not just bottling one particular vintage, there are multiple vintages.

They say grappa's an acquired taste because most people don't have good grappa. But if you have good grappa, it's not an acquired taste, it's a wonderful experience. Grappa is made from the skins of white grapes. We don't usually use the skins of white grapes in the manufacturing of a white wine, so all those sugars and those flavors stay in the skins and are normally discarded and composted. In the case of grappa, we save those skins, ferment those sugars out and distill that into a very soft, very clean, and aromatic spirit.

A good fruit spirit should tell the story of the fruit. The apples we use here are the old, tart apples, old-fashioned Winesaps, the Jonathan. Those are the base apples that we use. But we always like to blend in some sweet apple—never the majority—to add some of those sweet notes. We grow a lot of Galas, a lot of Golden Delicious here on the farm. We like to have some of those in our blend to let the fruit really, really express itself.

MAX TROYER

SECHLER'S PICKLES

Travel a few miles north of Fort Wayne, and you come to the little town of St. Joe, longtime home of Sechler's Pickles. Ralph Sechler started the business shortly before World War I, with his wife, Anna, who hand-packed Sechler's jars in the kitchen of their farmhouse. Today, that farmhouse serves as Sechler's headquarters, where Max Troyer, who grew up just a few miles away, now serves as Sechler's CEO. Sechler's uses cucumbers grown in northern Indiana, southern Michigan, and northwest Ohio to produce around forty-five different items, the majority of which are cured in cypress tanks. Sechler's distinctively flavored pickles serve as the inspiration for St. Joe's annual Pickle Festival, held in August. "People," says Troyer, "probably shouldn't be eating a hot dog without Sechler's relish on it."

{ *St. Joe* }

Caretaker of the brand

Going back years, we've kind of equated ourselves to the Ben & Jerry's of the pickle business. As far as unique products, that's really who we are.

We do a lot of unique flavors of pickles. We do an apple cinnamon flavor, we do an orange flavor, a lemon flavor, a raisin. As hot food has gotten bigger, we do some stuff with sweet and hot. We do some stuff with hot.

We use real sugar. It's considerably more expensive than high fructose corn syrup. And it's a lot harder to use than high fructose; it's not as efficient. It's heavy. You're lifting 100-pound bags, whereas with high fructose, you just pump it. It's a point of differentiation for us. Sugar definitely gets a different flavor profile.

We look a lot like a pickle company would have looked in 1950, 1960, before what

we call fresh-pack, or when your baby dills, spears, and bread-and-butter pickles became really popular.

There used to be a lot of what we call genuine dill or different flavor dills. So we do an orange flavor pickle, a dill sweet pickle, a candied sweet mix—that was the number one seller in those days. After the fifties and sixties, the industry changed. But we stayed in our own little niche here.

"It's a tough world. Pickles are one of those products that you either love or hate."

We could spend money on dill oil or dill flavor and not have a product that's any different than Vlasic or Mt. Olive. Whereas with the sugar, or in the flavors, there's a definite difference that people can discern.

Most of the pickle business is based in Michigan. We're relatively close to there. Yet, we're unique in that we're a pickle manufacturer in Indiana. There's only one other location that processes pickles in our state. At retail, we _are_ the pickle company.

They used to talk in our area about Eckrich Meats out of Fort Wayne, Seyfert's Potato Chips, County Line Cheese, and Sechler's Pickles. Well, we're the only ones left [owned locally].

I bought the company about four years ago from the family, and the way I look at it is you're kind of a caretaker of the brand. The big thing is to try and not screw it up. We have recognition issues, like do people really know what the company is? How many know that it's an Indiana business? We tend to have a little bit older consumer and so your worry is they pass on. You have to keep replenishing those customers with a younger group that knows and understands the brand.

It's a tough world. Pickles are one of those products that you either love or hate. There's not much in between. And there isn't like this eighteen-to-twenty-five demographic that's buying them. But the people that buy our pickles are important; they're a profitable part of the grocery market. Maintain, defend: For us that's Sechler's.

DAVID BARRICKMAN

WILDFLOWER RIDGE HONEY

David Barrickman of Wildflower Ridge Honey in Anderson is a fourth-generation beekeeper. A former president of the Indiana Beekeepers Association, Barrickman made raising honeybees his business after a thirty-seven-year career as an engineer for General Motors. Lately, Barrickman has focused on trying to replenish Indiana's diminishing honeybee population, which, he says, is stressed due what he calls "a concoction of chemicals that are now in the ground out there." Barrickman says that about 50 percent of the state's honeybees were lost in just one year. When we meet at a farmers' market where he's selling raw honey and other beehive products, including soaps and bee pollen, Barrickman says, "I'm not interested in producing a lot of honey. I'm more interested in making bees."

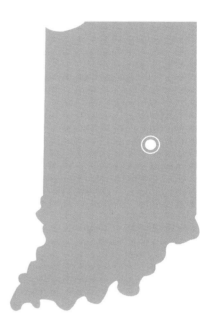

{Anderson}

God's medicine cabinet

I found out that my grandfather's father-in-law was a beekeeper. I learned that through a sale bill flyer that I found. When he passed away, they had a farm auction and there were two hives of bees listed in the auction.

My grandfather had bees for as long as I can remember. I was forty-six when he passed away at ninety-six. I really enjoyed being over at the farm and watching him catch swarms and put supers on and off—that's the top box on the beehive, where you get the honey from.

The one thing I always hated when I was a little kid was when we were out working bees I would get stung, and Grandpa chewed tobacco and he'd always spit on the sting. He said it helped, but I don't know. He said the tobacco juice would draw the poison out.

I enjoyed the whole biological aspect of the bees, the movement of them. Of course, I've gotten to know more about bees in the last fifteen to twenty years than I knew up to then. I really started studying and understanding the bees. In order to make it a business, you have to understand every aspect. If you don't know what's going on with your bees and inside your beehive and what seasons are bringing about for you, pretty soon you're out of business.

These honeybees are my employees.

"These honeybees are my employees."

They're just like dairy cattle in a barn. Those dairy cattle are making milk, and if they're not, that farmer wants to know why. That beehive is my barn and those bees are working for me. I want to make sure they're in full production.

In the summertime, when there's a nectar flow or the bees are working hard, the life expectancy of a worker bee is about forty-five days from the time it's born until the time it dies. They work themselves to death.

Consequently, you want good, fertile queens. A queen will lay anywhere between 1,500 and 2,000 eggs a day to keep the hive replenished. At the height of the nectar season, you want to have 60,000 to 80,000 bees in that beehive. When you come out in the springtime, that hive has dwindled down to 6,000 to 8,000. You have to build that hive up so it's ready for the nectar flow when it gets here.

My grandfather kept bees because he loved bees. He had thirty or forty hives around the farm. He never worried about selling honey. He practically gave it away. I used to carry it into work for him and sell it. He wouldn't even extract it; he just sold the frames, big honeycomb frames. He'd sell the whole thing for two bucks. Back then honey was about fifteen, twenty cents a pound. Today the retail price is six dollars a pound.

Granddad taught me a lot. He taught me patience, mainly.

Grandma passed away in 1919, during the swine flu epidemic that came through—he never remarried, and he raised his two boys and farmed his whole life. Patience was his virtue. He never got in a hurry, never got in a rush to do anything. He'd always think things out before we tackled something. He was a good teacher.

I went through a couple of phases in beekeeping. For years I wore a full suit and gloves and the veil—the whole thing. I had the bees out there and I worked them, but I didn't feel I was part of them. About twelve, fifteen years ago, I decided if I'm really going to get to know these bees, I'm just going to have to work them with no gloves. I took the gloves off and I never wear them when I work with bees. I get stung quite often. But it slows you down.

Before, when I wore the full gear, I would go in there and pull hives apart and throw this in that direction, pull honey out, and damage a lot of bees. When I quit wearing gloves, it slowed me down. I'm more patient. I'm slower. My observation time is much longer. I can inspect a beehive by just walking up to it and looking at it from the outside. Most people, when they open it up, all they see is bees. But I see bees, I see new nectar flows, I see brood, I see any type of disease I can recognize. Plus, I used to have some arthritic fingers and I don't have those arthritic fingers anymore. That's what we call bee venom therapy. A beehive's God's medicine cabinet, believe it or not.

STARTING OVER

"If somebody would have asked when I was going through high school what I was going to be, a pie maker would have been on the bottom of the list. I think God's got a good sense of humor."

LISA SPARKS

BERNADETTE OLIVIER AND ELIE LAURENT APOLLON

REFUGEE GARDENERS

{ *Fort Wayne* }

We met Bernadette and Elie on a misty morning at Catherine Kasper Place in Fort Wayne, a ministry sponsored by the Poor Handmaids of Jesus Christ, aimed at supporting services and opportunities for immigrants, refugees, and people seeking political asylum. The Haitian couple lost two sons in the 2010 earthquake.

Although neither had ever farmed before, they have learned the skills necessary to earn an income through the sale of their produce at local farmers' markets and churches. The first year, their crops were wiped out, but now their crops are thriving at several garden plots they tend in the area.

We take up the grass with our hands

Elie: I had trouble in Haiti. Before I came here, I am a businessman. I had a grocery store. I sell products, rice, and beans. I lived a better life. My family and me sometimes have a vacation in Europe or Canada, the Dominican Republic.

The trouble I had was they kidnapped me and my wife. I pay much money. The second time, they kidnapped my wife only. I pay $50,000. After that, I take my decision to move [some of] my family here. Me, I stay in Haiti. But after the earthquake, I move here to live with my family.

Bernadette: On January 12, 2010, the earthquake came. We lost everything: our business, our two boys, and house. Everything gone. He came here after the earthquake to see us, and when he came, I told him, "You can't go back: Stay." He said, "I can't." I said, "You don't have a choice; your family is here. You have to stay."

After that, we work at the First Assembly of God Church. Someone—her name is Brenda—talked to us. She asked us how we eat, sleep. She said she can help us. She paid the rent for us. And then, after that, I find a job. She had the ground, the little plot to grow.

We work the land. We brought tomatoes, peppers. She said, "Wow! You need a bigger plot?" We said yes.

Elie: In my country, any products is organic. I like organic products. Big difference. My sweet corn: organic. When you eat my sweet corn is very, very good. Now I have many beans, many sweet peppers. I have many hot peppers. We take up the grass with our hands.

Bernadette: We grow black-eyed peas at Dupont; the raccoons eat all. At New Haven, the raccoons eat sweet corn but not too much.

Elie: I'm very happy because this place connect us with many people. I have a big goal for my family: to open the first Caribbean restaurant in Fort Wayne.

BUD VOGT

BUD'S FARM MARKET

Down on the south side of Evansville, not far from the Ohio River, you find a part of town where city and country blur into one another. This is where Bud Vogt has his farm. Vogt, who sells his lovingly tended vegetables at farmers' markets, through independent groceries, and from a stand that has stood at the end of his driveway since he was a kid, has dedicated himself to preserving the farm where his parents and grandparents lived. "I want to stick with that tradition," he says.

{*Evansville*}

Vegas is for amateurs

The farm has been in the family for fifty-seven years. My grandfather was a farmer, a big corn and soybean farmer, and my father was a corn and soybean farmer. My father had health problems. At the time he farmed like 3,000 acres. But the doctor said, "You've got to slow down; you've got to look for something else to do."

So he started looking at vegetables. The first year he planted fifty tomato plants and 400 pounds of potatoes. As kids we sat out by the road trying to sell them.

Ellis Park is two miles away from us; it's a race park in Kentucky and, at that time, they were getting 8,000 to 10,000 cars a day, six days a week.

When the races let out, all this traffic was coming right by the farm. But things didn't take off for several years. It just took forever to get it going—and I hated it. In the middle of August it's so blasted hot, and humidity is so thick you can't walk. I swore I'd never have anything to do with the farm.

My father died in '77. But he had a guy that was working for him part time, and Mom said, "Here, you take care of it." So he took over the vegetable part. He really is the one who got us going. He could sell ice to Eskimos. He was a really good salesman, but he was a horrible farmer.

He died in 1995, and I was in Chicago, trading futures and options. I started having hearing problems and the doctor said I had to get off the trading floor. So I came back to Evansville to spend two or

"With farming I get that psychological fulfillment."

three years to take care of the farm and get it rebuilt and cleaned up. Well, two or three years has turned into sixteen years now.

Normally I do twenty, twenty-five varieties of tomatoes. We try and do the old-style heirlooms. Not only with tomatoes, but with everything: cucumbers, the peppers, the cantaloupe. We look for different varieties. Our key criterion is taste. We find that the older variety tomatoes, the heirlooms, tend to be better tasting than the newer varieties.

From what I'm told, with the newer varieties, to get a more uniform shape and to make the plant more disease resistant, to make it yield more per plant, they start playing with the genes. But that also impacts the flavor. So while they're developing a tomato that yields twenty pounds per plant, that can be thrown against the side of a barn and not dent the tomato, that can sit in a truck in a cardboard box, and travel a thousand miles of constant shaking, and then sit on the grocery shelf for two weeks, with people picking them up and putting them down, when they make the tougher tomato, they also lose the flavor.

My philosophy and my mindset is that we got to change the way that we grow and supply food in this country. Basically, we are growing our food supply in two deserts: Florida and across through Texas and out west, where they're shipping water in. After they ship the water in, they ship the food back across the country. That's got to stop. I think we have to grow our food on a more regional basis and shorten the transportation cost, as well as deal with irrigation.

When I was in the corporate world, I was making considerably more money than I do now. But I was living in the big city and it was harried and just a different lifestyle. To a degree, I miss some of that. There's so much more to do in a big city. But, at the same time, even though I was doing relatively well financially, there was still an emptiness or something that was missing. With farming I get that psychological fulfillment. I'm more directly related to benefiting society and having a positive impact on the community, on the environment.

But it sure would be nice to be making a little more money. I was at the Board of Trade, I was at the Mercantile Exchange, and I was at the Options Exchange. I was in New York for a while and actually turned down a transfer to New York. That's a different kind of stress. And, actually, I guess I didn't understand it at the time—I was too young—but my father used to say that Vegas was for amateurs. If you really wanted to take a risk or gamble, get into farming.

NICK BOYD

SOUTH SIDE SODA SHOP AND DINER

When we take a booth in Goshen's South Side Soda Shop and Diner, we can't help but notice the way the guy in the Phillies cap behind the counter converses with a little girl who's having a bite to eat. He asks her about her homework, and she happily tells him about her latest assignment. This sort of conversation is the kind of everyday pleasure Nick Boyd and his family serve up along with their original take on diner fare at this restored neighborhood gem. The restaurant is festooned with vintage pennants and a time-bending array of period memorabilia, including a working 1940s Bastian-Blessings soda fountain. But the real sense of timelessness comes in the way Boyd and the rest of the crew relate to customers of all ages.

{ *Goshen* }

Loving the neighborhood

This has a long history, this soda shop. Originally, in 1910, when it opened up, it was a grocery store, called Dean's Grocery. Then, in 1942, a couple bought it, Junior and Evie Kirkdorfer, and turned it into the South Side Soda Shop.

Evie and Junior had retired and the place was closed. They're both deceased now, but Evie was a big fan. She would come in weekly, wearing her Soda Shop T-shirt and was proud the restaurant was still in operation.

My wife, Charity, is from Detroit, and I'm from Philadelphia. Our parents were antique dealers; they were friends doing business together, and they introduced us. We got married and were living in Philadelphia, but then my wife's dad retired here in Goshen. He bought this building and was restoring it. Then we helped with the restoration, bought the building from him, and opened up the restaurant. We were expecting our first child and thought Goshen would be a nice place to bring up a family. That was twenty-six years ago!

We ended up loving the neighborhood so much that we bought the house right behind the restaurant. Our children went to Parkside Elementary School right next

"It's a lot of fun to cook and have people enjoy what you make and create."

door and would come over here right after school. They've grown up here. Our neighbors walk here for lunch, dinner.

Four doors away is a family named the Smuckers. Their three boys all walked here. One, Benjie, used to tell his teachers that he was going home for lunch and stop in here instead. Well, now, Benjie's my doctor!

When we were putting the menu together, most of it was what we enjoyed eating and family recipes. Philadelphia influenced us a lot. I make snapping-turtle soup. That was real popular in Philadelphia, in the seafood restaurants. I get all my fish and shellfish out of Chicago, fresh, and I asked them to find turtle meat for me. I started making it about four years ago, and it's so popular that we have it every day now. I just kept tweaking it until it brought back memories.

Twenty-six years ago, most of the restaurants that were in Goshen were not chains. I mean we had a McDonald's, an Arby's. But they were family run, and we wanted to create our own niche and not try to steal the customers from another place. How many pork tenderloins or hamburgers can there be?

So we make as much from scratch as we can or get it locally. I've got a Sunday school group coming in this evening (they come in every month), so I asked them: What would you like next month? Meatloaf is the plan for tonight. It's my mother's recipe.

Today I got fresh basil, so we're making our pesto. We do that a couple of times a week.

All our pies are made from scratch. I used to do it, but then our eldest daughter, Nicole, graduated from Goshen College. She was working here, and I was looking for something to make it a little more interesting for her than just waiting on tables—not that there's anything wrong with that, because that's how I started out. But she took over the baking a little over three years ago, and I think she does a wonderful job. She was here before I was this morning. They did a yearlong pie quest, the Indiana Pie Quest. Our lemon meringue pie was picked best pie in Indiana.

I had no experience cooking but found sort of a passion for it. It's a lot of fun to cook and have people enjoy what you make and create. We get people that came in when the Kirkdorfers were here and people in their fifties that attended Parkside Elementary School or Goshen College and are bringing their children in to show them where they used to hang out.

Years ago, we had people wanting to know if we would sell the soda fountain and some of the memorabilia and antiques, but we're not ready to quit yet. Hopefully, my daughter will keep it going. We're still having too much fun. I get a kick, if the school crossing guard can't show up, going out and crossing the kids. This is a real neighborhood. It's important to me.

GUSTAVO RODRIGUEZ AND YALILI MESA

CALIENTE CUBAN CUISINE

Every day, Gustavo ("Gus," to his many friends) Rodriguez posts a Spanish word on the wall of Caliente Cuban Cuisine, the Cuban restaurant he operates with his wife, Yalili, in Fort Wayne. If you can translate the word, you get a free side. "I was searching for the really hard words in Spanish," laughs Gus. "That's a tradition here that we have: every day, a different word. I'm teaching for free!" In a little over four years, Caliente Cuban Cuisine has become a popular destination for people with a craving for the flavors of authentic Cuban street food—and the Rodriguez's generous hospitality.

{ Fort Wayne }

My teachers are my customers

Gustavo: I was a refugee. I was a journalist in Cuba and I belonged to this independent group of journalists; seventy-five of us went to jail. Once, Castro talked to the whole nation, and he mentioned my name. If Castro mentions your name, you're in trouble.

I call a friend living here. She was a journalist with me in Cuba, and she say, "Welcome to Fort Wayne!" I didn't know where Fort Wayne was, but I got a job with the Community Harvest Food Bank. I work there for seven years and thought I'd retire.

But my wife was looking for something to do, and she found this place. She say, "Hey, Gus, I'm going to open a restaurant."

Yalili: I like cooking, but I never think of cooking for other people. I turned to my husband: "We need to do something."

Gustavo: She opened it by herself. All the fame, all the glory, is to her, for sure. She opened it and stayed here seven or eight months by herself. It was so busy.

Yalili: I learn English here. This is my school! This restaurant. I didn't speak at all three years ago. I was really scared to answer the phone. Gus came. He say, "You got orders by phone?" I say, "No. Nobody called …"

Sopa!
Mtn Dew for $0.75
(20 OZ.)
WE APPRECIATE YOUR Business.
Credit Card Transaction: $5.00 OR MORE

"If Castro mentions your name, you're in trouble."

Gustavo: She lied to me. People called, but she didn't answer.

Yalili: The ring was off, you know? The ring was off. I tell him, "No. Nobody called." He say, "Yalita (he call me Yalita like I was a girl), the ring is off." I say, "I'm sorry. I'm scared."

Gustavo: She didn't get the calls. She hung up.

Yalili: It took three or four months. I tell the people, "Please, talk to me slowly." Now I got it. With my accent and everything, but I got it. The customers have really big patience. My teachers are my customers.

Gustavo: You can buy Cuban sandwiches here in Fort Wayne at other places. But they make them with other breads, and it doesn't look the same and it doesn't taste the same. The bread is the secret. It is the key. The roasted pork could be anywhere. It is not a secret.

No, it's the bread. We make the bread here. Cuban bread is very easy. You know, we are Spain's children, but Cuban bread is more like French bread. Our kitchens have a lot of French culinary influence. For our breakfast, we do not eat like you or like Spain.

We eat like the French—French toast and *café con leche*. That's what we eat. It's interesting. We inherit some French culinary things. We use a lot of butter, like the French.

We don't have a lot of competitors. I think in Indy there's a Cuban restaurant by the Circle and that's it in the whole state of Indiana. What is funny is after we open this restaurant, some restaurants in town start making Cuban sandwiches. They stop already. People say, "No, if I want a Cuban sandwich, I go to Caliente."

People come here from all around the world. They look in the Urbanspoon, and they come here. And people come from Illinois, from Ohio, just to eat our sandwiches.

Yalili: We have customers who eat our sandwiches and say, "Oh, my God, we drive for hours just to come here."

Gustavo: I appreciate that so much because, for me, it is a big surprise. People come here from Australia, from China. I'm going to start building a list, a visitor's book. I went to college in Cuba where we had people from a lot of countries, and I thought I would never have that experience again. Wrong!

DAVE FISCHER

FISCHER FARMS

Dave Fischer raises natural, high-quality beef on about 700 acres of hilly, wooded country outside Jasper. His great-great grandfather bought the first piece of land from the local sheriff because the farmer who owned it never returned from the Civil War. Dave was born and raised here but came to farming after a successful career as an engineer and computer software designer in Texas and, for a time, in Germany. "When I moved back," he recalls, "I said if I'm going to raise cattle, I want to raise really good cattle." Dave's herd is fed an all-vegetarian diet, with no added hormones or antibiotics. The meat is aged for fourteen days to enhance the flavor. It is tenderized by being hung in a temperature-controlled environment so that natural enzymes break down the muscle fibers. This attention to detail has associated the Fischer Farms brand with quality in restaurants throughout Indiana.

{*Jasper*}

This is my office today

I've always really enjoyed agriculture. I would cry when my dad wouldn't take me along outside when I was four and five years old. But I felt when I was growing up that there wouldn't be that many opportunities in agriculture. I think that's changed.

I'm a big believer that people need to understand where their food comes from, what's the process. I think if a lot of people understood where some of their food comes from today, they would really be upset. I was talking to a guy at a food show who used to work in poultry, but they didn't process chickens. They got what they called "the white slime," which was this processed meat. It was basically a liquefied meat they got off the bones, and they would basically dry it and form it and turn it into chicken nuggets and send it to the schools. If people understood that, I think there'd be a big call to have some changes in how our food's grown.

With calves, probably the most important thing is the genetics of the animal. That really determines the quality of the meat. The next is how they're treated and how they're cared for. What I don't want to see is a skinny calf at three months of age that's not getting enough nutrition,

"But I felt when I was growing up that there wouldn't be that many opportunities in agriculture. I think that's changed."

not growing properly. We make sure the cows always have a nice green-blush diet in front of them. We try to rotate pastures about every two weeks so there's always good grass for them to eat, then we'll supplement that with hay, what we call haylage, which is just wet, baled hay. That ferments and makes a good, dense energy for the cows.

It's genetics, it's feed as they're a calf and then it's feed while they're going through the growth stage.

If you take care of the calf at about sixteen to eighteen months old, they're ready to butcher. If you have time periods in there where they're not getting enough energy and if you have them on bad pasture or poor quality hay and they're not growing then, all of a sudden, it's twenty months old, or twenty-four months old before they're ready to butcher, and that's when you get the poor quality ones.

So it's knowing when the calf was born, taking care of the calf all the way through, and then you have to start off with the right bull and the right cow to produce the calf. Those seem to be the critical things.

Today is a nice day to be outside, but two days ago, when it rained all day and it was cold, was not a good day to be outside for those calves. If they're in those barns, we keep sawdust underneath them and we keep it dry—both to keep them healthy but also to keep them comfortable. They're lying down and they're not stressed out, feeling like they have to be standing or cold or hot.

When I was raising a family, I wanted to bring the kids back and have them in a very stable environment during their middle school and high school years. It's easy to transport a kid into different schools when they're in the second grade and third grade, but, after that, you need to start settling them down. We also wanted to be close to the grandparents.

I also hated it when I was in the computer world, and I'd come home and the kids would say, "What did you do today?" What do you tell them? I was in meetings. I was in meetings talking about computer algorithms. That's pretty well the end of the conversation.

Now, I can tell them, hey, here's what we do—and they're involved in it. All my kids have been heavily involved in both the farm aspect as well as selling the meat. We take them to farmers' markets. They know the chefs. They really understand what we do, and I think it's been a great learning experience for them.

I definitely agree that beef is a resource that you just can't produce an endless amount of. You can't do like chickens, where you can put them in big buildings, and the size of the building determines how much you can raise. With beef you have to have land. You have to have open space for them. I love it when I'm talking to a chef or somebody on my cell phone. I'll take a picture of where I'm standing, and I'll say, "This is my office today."

LISA SPARKS

LISA'S PIE SHOP

For over twenty-three years, Lisa Sparks and her husband, Jim, have been making prize-winning pies at the intersection of Highway 31 and County Line Road in Atlanta. People love Lisa's pies so much that, during the holidays, a local police officer has been assigned to direct traffic off the highway into Lisa's parking lot. Lisa makes at least twenty-three different types of pies and continues to develop recipes that have won her blue ribbons in competitions with chefs from around the country. An Indiana Artisan, she has also become known for her Pie in a Jar line. "I never went to cooking school," she says. "If somebody would have asked when I was going through high school what I was going to be, a pie maker would have been on the bottom of the list. I think God's got a good sense of humor."

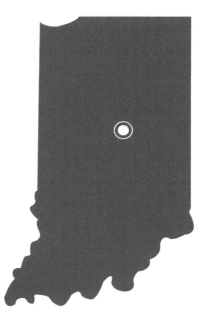

{ *Atlanta* }

I don't like pie

I put it like this: God picks the least likely one, so everybody knows it's God. Well, he picked me. I don't like pie. I've never tried most of my pies. I'm just not a pie eater.

Making pies was not a dream, okay? It was a way to get out of the factory. I worked at Paint and Assembly Corporation. We did bumpers for GM. And, at twenty-nine, I found out that I had cancer and realized

that life was too short to go someplace you didn't want to go.

All I know is I tried to impress my husband in my younger years. He was a farm boy, and his mom is one of the greatest cooks I've ever met. He is the second greatest.

So I used to try and impress him. I had been trying to make pies when his best friend's mom put her arm around me one

day and said, "Oh, honey, if you just put this and this in your pie crust and this and this in your filling, you'll never have a bad pie again."

And she was right. I've never had a bad pie since.

Then, I guess, what made me start the pie shop was the girls I worked with at the factory entered me in this apple pie

"What they didn't understand was I didn't like pie anyway, so they couldn't hurt my feelings."

contest. I won grand champion! Never made an apple pie before. Don't even like pie! But when I won grand champion, a little light bulb went off in my head. It was like, "Hmmm, I could do this."

That's what started it.

I took questionnaires to my neighbors, to my local beauty shop, to anybody I could get to try pies. They would tell me what I needed to do. The worst part about it was getting people to tell you the truth, because they thought they would hurt my feelings. What they didn't understand was I didn't like pie anyway, so they couldn't hurt my feelings. I really needed them to tell me the truth. Once I got them convinced of that, they did.

You know, women don't cook anymore, and, if they do cook, it usually comes from a box. So when somebody tells me that the pies taste like what their mom used to make, or their grandmother, then I know I'm on the right track, because here we truly still do everything by hand. Everything is fresh.

Nothing comes from a box.

A lot of people find this odd, but I never count how many pies I have to do. It would shake me up if I did. It would make me tired before I even got started. I learned a long time ago not to psych myself out, so I don't count. But then, when it's all said and done, especially at Thanksgiving, Christmas, and we really stop and think about how many people's houses we're sitting in, how many people we touch during that time, it's kind of awesome.

I can remember my first big order was twenty-five pies and it took me twenty-seven hours. Now twenty-five pies takes me about a half hour. Twenty-five hundred to do in a day or two is when I start getting shook up. But, like I said, I quit counting a long time ago.

I am very proud of Pie in a Jar. It came about because we didn't let pies sit more than twenty-four hours. We didn't want those pies to go to waste, so we began canning them. My husband comes from a long line of canning. His mom canned everything. They even dug stuff out of the yard that I thought you put weed killer on, you know what I mean?

But my mother and grandparents also canned. It took us about five years to learn how to can those pies and to make them shelf-stable for six to eight months. The funny thing is when we started, we used leftover pies. But we don't have leftover pies anymore. Very rarely do we have a pie left, so we had to learn to do them without making pie. And people love it. A lot of them say it's better than the pie itself.

I'm very, very lucky, very blessed because we get to come to work and we get complimented every single day. Somewhere down the line during the day, somebody will say something nice to us about the pies. Rarely do you go to a job and get complimented every single day. God was so good to me that he didn't just give me a pie shop. He gave me an award-winning pie shop. I think he expected me to do everything I could to help other people, so he gave me a venue where I could bless people, and people could bless me.

WARREN AND JILL SCHIMPFF

SCHIMPFF'S CONFECTIONERY

When Warren Schimpff was a kid, he'd leave his home in Chicago to visit his grandparents, aunts, uncles, and cousins in Jeffersonville, on the Ohio River. For young Warren, Jeffersonville was a sweet retreat; his grandparents owned and operated a candy store and soda fountain where they made candy and ice cream by hand. Warren learned to make the candy himself.

After Warren grew up, he married his childhood sweetheart, Jill, received a PhD in environmental chemistry, and eventually settled out west. While they were in California, the Schimpffs collected antique candy-making equipment like that found in the family's shop. Warren began making sweets in his garage.

During this time, Warren's aunt was running the shop. When she passed away in 1989, Warren and Jill bought Schimpff's and then, for ten years, shuttled back and forth, between California and Jeffersonville, to keep it going. Finally, in 2000, the couple retired and returned to Jeffersonville in order to run the business. Today, Schimpff's Confectionary includes a 2,500-square-foot museum with what may be the largest collection of confectionary memorabilia on public display in the United States. The business recently celebrated its 120th anniversary. Warren and Jill live upstairs, in the same rooms where Warren's father was born in 1928.

{ Jeffersonville }

A little taste, a little pleasure

Warren: I love making candy so people can see it, see the way it was done in the old days. There's just nothing like this in the country, the type of demonstration we do here.

Jill: The candy has a personality because of the people that are here making it. We get lots of people that are interested in the way things are made, especially children.

Warren: When I was a kid and we came down here, it was generally past candy season. If you step back in time and think about before there was air-conditioning, you couldn't make candy in the summertime. Candy was a wintertime activity. A candy shop like this could only make candy in the fall. Thinking of chocolate, you couldn't have chocolate in the shop unless it was cold outside. And with the humidity problems you get with hard candy … before there was air-conditioning and dehumidifiers, you had to wait until your environment got dry before you could have candy for sale.

"That's the kind of thing we'd like to continue here: Give everybody a little taste, a little pleasure."

So the candy season was usually October through Easter. A shop like this, typically, had a wintertime business and a summertime business. The summertime business was ice cream.

People come here for generations. We get grandmothers that will come in with their grandkids and tell the grandchild, well, you know, in that back booth over there, I had my first date. In the thirties and forties, this was basketball central for the city of Jeffersonville. People would gather here for ice cream after the games. We had one of the few telephones in downtown Jeffersonville, and when there would be away games, somebody would call the pay phone here and give the scores. They would paint them quickly on the front window as people drove by.

Jill: And there's probably not many people in town that don't have somebody in their family that worked here at one point.

Warren: You should understand that we go back to grade school together. Some of our earlier dates, we would come down here together and help the family.

Jill: We had one man come by, and he said, "Warren, I have a great story about your Aunt Catherine." He said he was a little kid with his nose pressed against the glass by the chocolate drops and she said, "I bet you'd like one of those, wouldn't you?"

He said, "Yes, ma'am."

She said, "How much money do you have?"

He said, "Just enough to get into the LaRose Theatre."

She said, "Well, all right then." And she snapped open a little brown bag and put in three chocolate drops and said, "Here." Then she snatched it back and said, "You don't tell anybody where you got these."

And he said, "No ma'am."

So he's in the theater, sitting on his chocolate, and he's thinking, this is a bad idea. He took it out and started eating and a little boy next to him said, "Where'd you get that?"

And he said, "I can't tell."

And the other little kid said, "Oh, she gave us all some."

That's the kind of thing we'd like to continue here: Give everybody a little taste, a little pleasure.

Warren: We took this on with the idea that we wanted to keep some family history alive, we wanted to keep candy history alive, and we wanted to see what we could do with Spring Street—whether we could make an impact on the community. Nobody's going to remember me for what I did in the chemistry business, my water analysis. But my candy-making tenure here had quite an impact on the city of Jeffersonville and Spring Street. In 1990, when we re-opened the business, you could almost shoot a cannonball down the street and not hit anything. Today, there's quite a bit of activity, and we'd like to think we've had a portion of something to do with that. I know we have.

MARIA GONZALEZ

FORMER MIGRANT WORKER

Maria Gonzalez lives with her husband and children in a suburban-style house in Walton, Indiana. Maria was a so-called "anchor baby," born in Texas to Mexican parents who brought her back to live in the United States when she was a teenager. Maria and her family worked in the fields in Texas and in Florida before settling in Indiana, where she's made her home ever since. Hers is a classic American story of hard work and self-improvement. But, it turns out, Maria's dream is to return to Mexico, where she and her husband own land and are building a house. "My husband will be farming and I will be helping him," says Maria. "That's the plan."

{ *Walton* }

You work long hours

It was back in '83 and my dad used to work for this company that did landscaping. While he was working here during the summer, we were back in Mexico. Then, when we got older, my dad says, "Okay, it's time for you guys to come and join me." So he went and got us and we came here.

I was thirteen or fourteen years old. I came not knowing the language, and it was very difficult. I remember that we came in May—I'll never forget that—and we started working out in the fields right away.

We started with planting tomatoes and then, after that, cleaning the tomatoes, hoeing. It was getting up early in the morning and my mom fixing us something to eat. It was all day. We were usually getting home around six o'clock or seven. In summer, it gets late.

When planting the tomatoes was over, we did the corn detasseling. Then August came and we harvested tomatoes. It was very, very hard because you were always on your knees. We picked the tomatoes

and put them into baskets. Now they have machines, but before that it was hard.

The first year we came here, we went to Florida to work because my dad said that during winter it gets too cold here and he gets laid off. He knew a friend that told him in Florida there was a lot of agriculture work, so we went to Florida. We were picking the strawberries and the green tomatoes, grapefruit, oranges.

We came back in the spring. My dad says, "We're not going anywhere; we're just

"He said, 'Yeah, but you have to try. You keep trying and you'll get it.'"

going to stay here in Indiana." He didn't want to take us out of school, back and forth, and we never moved again.

Oh, I didn't want to go to school. That was the hardest part because of the language. But we were lucky enough that we had good teachers and they helped us.

I started sixth grade. I was only in class for math, plus PE and music and art. The rest of the day I was with another teacher who was teaching me the language. That helped me a lot because I was the only one and she was only teaching me.

The kids in that school were nice. We never had any problems. We always had nice people and nice teachers who were willing to try and communicate with me.

But the winters were terrible. We got several storms and were out of electricity for a few days. All we did was cry and cry. We wanted to go back to Mexico because of the winter and the language. We kept telling my dad, "We're never going to learn English; it's so difficult!" He said, "Yeah, but you have to try. You keep trying and you'll get it."

So we did. Then we stopped doing the agricultural work, and I started working at McDonald's. I was probably seventeen. After that, I graduated from high school.

I graduated in '91 and worked as a teacher's aide. While I did that, I had a second job at Hometown Pizza. Then I moved to the Logansport Community Schools, and that's when I started working for the state with migrant families. I worked for the state for thirteen years, but my position was cut.

Now, you don't see that many people coming. I'm going to say maybe it's because of the economy and immigration issues—people just don't want to travel like they used to. And they use machines for the tomatoes; they don't hire that many people. They only need so many to run the machine. Before, when it was just picking the tomatoes, they would need extra hands.

I still have some growers that call me and say, "Do you know of any migrants who want to work?" There's a person who hires lots of school kids to do the detasseling. He's always calling me.

We [migrant workers] do the work without asking many questions. Like if they said, "Okay, you're going to get $5.50 an hour," we're like, "OK. I need the money, so I need to work."

And you work long hours.

When I talked to migrant families, I was always trying to help them before they would go to another state. They finish whatever work is here and then go to Michigan to harvest apples or move to New York or to Washington or Florida. Usually the ones that come through Indiana go from here to Michigan, then to Florida and from Florida, back again to Indiana. It's with the seasons. When we did it that first time, I didn't like it. We only moved once; that was enough.

THE GOODS

"I tell people who work here that as soon as something is picked, it's got a time clock on it."

MARCUS AGRESTA

MARCUS AGRESTA
PIAZZA PRODUCE

If you live anywhere near Indianapolis—or in parts of Illinois, Ohio, or Kentucky, for that matter—you have probably seen a Piazza Produce truck making the rounds in your town. Now based on the north side of Indianapolis, Piazza Produce has grown from a south side produce stand into a large-scale, twenty-four-hour operation, with a fleet of refrigerated trucks carrying volumes of fresh food from cavernous warehouse facilities. Marcus Agresta, Piazza's director of sales and marketing, led us through enormous spaces, where workers loaded forklifts with pallets stacked with peppers, peaches, and cheese.

{*Indianapolis*}

Balancing act

My father-in-law, Pete Piazza, started this business in 1970. Both his parents and grandparents were in the produce business. Back then, it was a driving-down-the-street, peddler scenario; as a little boy, he grew up around that.

He started a produce stand on the south side. He had one truck and, at that time, the tomatoes he was getting were also from the south side.

In those days, something was happening in the marketplace—people were crunched for time and the fast food industry started to proliferate. There was a Burger Chef down the street from his stand, and he called on them and said, "Hey, I've got this produce here at my stand. How about I take care of your needs?"

So he took care of that guy, and that guy told another guy, and before you knew it, there were several Burger Chefs around town buying his produce. Hard work and timing paid off.

It used to be that people—chefs, especially—wanted to get things from as far away as possible. They wanted a lychee nut or a new variety of something from South Africa. Now they're trying to get things from as close as possible. That's the cornerstone of what we're seeing right now.

It's going to be up to us to help the producers understand what we need. For example, we have a grower we've been doing some business with for the past five years. He never grew squash, but this year

"I tell people who work here that as soon as something is picked, it's got a time clock on it."

he's growing squash. We never bought squash from Indiana before; we always bought it from Michigan because nobody grew it here. People would say they saw squash at the farmers' market; well, yeah, but they don't understand what it takes: We need pallets of squash. Maybe they saw 100 pounds, but I get 100 pounds with just three orders. So it's up to us to work with people, to plan and talk about what we need.

I think a lot of farmers start out trying to make their own deliveries. They soon realize this is a lot of work. They're driving all these miles, and they're only delivering three of their things. Fischer Farms in southern Indiana used to do that. He made his own meat deliveries. Then he approached us, we got to know each other, and we've taken over everything for him. That lets him concentrate on what he does best, which is raise the product and cut it and talk to the customers about what they want, instead of being in the vehicle all the time.

One of the keys is having the fleet. Our refrigerated trucks give us the tentacles to be very flexible. If you've got a guy in Terre Haute who's growing something, we can pick the stuff up tomorrow because we've got ten trucks going by there. We can pop off, grab it, and go.

I tell people who work here that as soon as something is picked, it's got a time clock on it and it's starting to break down. It's a balancing act. We've got to have enough to sell, but we can't have too much to throw away. We carry 3,000 items, and half of them are perishable. We're not selling vacuum cleaners; they're not made on an assembly line. God's the boss: the weather, the weather, the weather.

We were challenged three or four years ago by a chef who was very adamant about local food. I got an email from him and it said, "What's a big business like Piazza Produce doing about supporting the local food economy?" It pissed me off because we've been buying local since Pete founded the business. We just never marketed the fact we did it because we didn't know people wanted to know that.

Since then, we talk about our story, and telling our story has evolved into a separate marketing web site, where we have profiles on all our local producers, whether it's the goat cheese we get, the kale we get from the south side, or the tomatoes from up in Fayetteville. We're a family-owned business. We're not big business. It was eye-opening that if you don't tell people what you do, you can't assume that they know.

It's funny: Now that chef and I are pretty good friends.

KIM ROBINSON

TWO COOKIN' SISTERS

North of Lafayette, Highway 421 runs through the town of Brookston. At the intersection there, you'll find a busy corner market that, in lipstick red letters, proclaims itself to be the home of Two Cookin' Sisters. The sisters, Kim Robinson and Kristi Robinson Rensberger, have been in business for over ten years. What started with homemade salsa has evolved into one of the state's best retail outlets for handcrafted and artisanal products bearing the Made in Indiana label. The Robinson's Brookston homestead dates back to 1852. "This wasn't what I thought it was going to be," says Robinson, "but I knew it was time to do something different."

{ *Brookston* }

Made in Indiana

I had just moved back from California, and I wanted to send made-in-Indiana items to my friends in California because when I lived there I sent made-in-California items to my friends in Indiana. They had jams and wines and chutneys and the tapenades. I mean there was just store after store with all this stuff!

Then, when I moved back to Indiana, I was looking for this same kind of thing, and there really wasn't anything available. In Indianapolis, at Circle Centre Mall, there was a store that was all made in Indiana, but it was going out of business. I thought, why isn't this taking off? Why isn't this happening?

My sister had created this salsa. We were making it for friends and family. Then, finally, after a year of giving it away, we had neighbors who said, "You know, you ought to put a label on this and sell it." So that's what we did. We made our first batch of 200 jars and printed our labels off on our computer and went to one of the craft bazaars in northern Indiana.

And we sold all 200 jars.

At that point we knew we had something. But both of us were working full time, and we didn't have the ability to cook the salsa and sell it, so we found someone to make it for us. In 2001, we introduced Big Sister Salsa at the Brookston Apple Popcorn Festival. About 750 jars. We sold out that day.

Come 2004, 2005, we were making other

products. We were renting a kitchen and making apple butter, a couple of jams, and some other items. And my mom said, "You girls really need your own kitchen because renting a kitchen, you're really not making any money." So we found this location and it had a kitchen.

We weren't thinking about doing the retail part of it, but then we had found a lot of small companies that were making products and needed a place to sell them. Like us, they were too small to buy shelves at the big grocery stores. If you had something you wanted to sell, we weren't going to charge you a shelf rental, you could bring your stuff in, and we'd put a Made in Indiana sticker on it. We were getting phone calls from people saying, "I'd like to sell my product in your store. We cook on the weekends. We don't have a lot of inventory, but we'd like to get it out on the market."

I grew up on a farm. I know how things are grown. I know where things come from. But you've got a lot of kids that don't have that exposure. It's not part of their curriculum. They don't know where things come from or what they look like. We sell popcorn that's on the ear, and people are fascinated by that. They don't know that's what it looks like before it goes in the bag, so they buy it up. I can't keep it on the shelf. Simple popcorn that, as kids, we used to grind it off the ear and put it in a big jar. That

was our popcorn! Now these people think it's such a novelty, and I just think that's crazy.

There're a lot of people that pass through Brookston to get to wherever they're going. I'd say 80 percent of our business is people passing through. They'll come from northwest Indiana. They'll pick up I-65 down here, or they like taking 421 because they don't want to deal with I-65. We have people from Chicago, and then there are people coming up from Indianapolis on their way to Lake Michigan.

At one time, when the recession was really tough in 2008, it was very scary. There were lots of things happening that we didn't have answers for and neither did anybody else. My dad said it best. He said, "You've got a lot of people who rely on you. You've got to figure it out. You can't just close up shop and go home and say that's it. You've got people that rely on that paycheck, and you've got a community that relies on you to keep that corner going." Those were the best words of advice. What I'm most proud of is being able to get through that.

We've come out on the other side. I think growing things locally and buying locally is only going to get stronger. People are starting to understand how important it is for the money to stay in their own community, to go to someone they know.

LARRY WAPPEL

WAPPEL FARMS

Drive Highway 421 between San Pierre and North Judson after a rainstorm in July and, if you're lucky, you'll smell the aroma of fresh peppermint. Larry Wappel is a third-generation farmer who has been growing mint and distilling the oil since 1988. Of the 60,000 acres devoted to mint in the United States, about 15,000 acres are found in northwest Indiana. "I like challenges," says Wappel. "I like to see if I can grow something different. So I started working on the mint farms one summer for something to do and liked what I saw. I thought I could do this." Wappel says farmers are also fabricators: He has built much of his own specialized mint farming gear—diggers, planters, and steam distillation equipment, including separators, and condensers—in his shop.

{ *San Pierre* }

Mint in the air

Mint was brought into northwest Indiana in the late twenties or early thirties by two pretty big farm families because of the organic soils we have. The muck soils are very high in organic; they are fluffy, loose; they're not a clay or a tight soil. If we try to grow it in tight clay soils or the prairie soils, like you have in central Illinois or down in central or southern Indiana, it will not do so well. The roots have to be able to penetrate the soil.

There are only a few spots in the nation like this, and one of them happens to be here, in the Kankakee River Basin.

We also have more varying microclimates because of Lake Michigan. That's why you see the grapes and the apples and cherries. Here we still catch the lake effect; it preserves our roots. Mint's a perennial; the roots are living organisms for next year's crop, so we love to see snow and we get a lot more snow here in winter.

I have 1,200 acres of spearmint and peppermint, about 200 acres of native spearmint, which is completely different. It's the mint family, but it's the spearmint family, so when we distill that, we have to keep it separate, totally separate. If I saw a spearmint plant in my peppermint field, I'd pull it out and get rid of it. It has its own special uses, and there's a small need for it, but most mint farmers in Indiana don't even mess with it.

"Most mint goes back to Wrigley's and Colgate."

Most mint goes back to Wrigley's and Colgate. It's a mainstay for toothpaste and mouthwashes, as far as Colgate-Palmolive goes. Then, of course, Wrigley's is candies and gums. There's also a small amount that goes to liqueur companies for things like peppermint schnapps.

When Wrigley's has a gum, let's say Doublemint Gum, they want Doublemint Gum to be the same from year to year to year. So our oil is going to be very similar each year, but not perfectly similar because we have different weather from year to year. The buyer-broker's job is to buy oil—say, from the Midwest—and then squeeze in some cheap oil from India or China and still meet Wrigley's specs for that year. Just like there's a recipe for any food, there is a recipe for Wrigley's for a specific mint oil, and it's got to be consistent.

We have probably the most desirable oil. If you're going to use oil for blending purposes, you want ours on the top of the line to blend with. In the United States, we have Midwest oil. The Midwest oil is grown in southern Michigan, northwest Indiana, and in parts of Wisconsin. We're in the right latitude and longitude for that. Then there's the Far West oil, which is grown in Washington, Oregon, Idaho. They have a totally different climate, and the oils have different chemical makeups that look completely different from our oil.

When buyers first get a sample of our oil, they're like wine tasters. They'll take a little swizzle stick and they'll dip it in each sample. Then they'll take it in a little glass and they'll hold it up to the light to see what color it has, how clear it is. They grade it according to their taste and the smell, and the color, and then they'll run it through the gas chromatograph and grade it for purity.

The neat thing is this variety of peppermint goes back at least eighty or ninety years in Indiana and, before that, it was brought from Europe and settled in Pennsylvania for a while. That's where the Black Mitcham variety we grow actually came from.

There are little, bitty microscopic oil glands on the bottom sides of the leaves. There's no oil on the stem; there's no oil on the topsides of the leaves. It's all down below. Just walking through it, we're rupturing those little oil glands. So right after a big storm, if the wind comes through here, it'll blow the mint, and they'll rub on each other and break the oil glands. Then you'll have a real strong smell of mint in the air.

CARL GARWOOD

GARWOOD ORCHARD

Carl Garwood, one of the patriarchs of Garwood Orchard, greets us in the cool shade of the production facility attached to his family's market and U-pick operation in LaPorte. Now that a younger generation is taking over the day-to-day management of the business, Garwood may claim to be "semiretired," but he's still trim, still wearing his cap and jeans.

The Garwoods have farmed in this part of northwest Indiana for generations; now the Garwood family raises a dazzling array of fruits and vegetables, including apples, peaches, raspberries, pumpkins, strawberries, cherries, sweet corn, and cucumbers. Asked to describe his job, Garwood simply says: "Trying to make things grow well."

{*LaPorte*}

The best place for an apple orchard

Our history started here in 1832. That was when the land was bought from the state for fifty cents an acre. There were some Indians around here at that time. Anyway, that's what my great-great-grandfather said.

Most farms back at the turn of the century had cows, chickens, hogs, grain, a home orchard—a little bit of everything because we lived off the farm. My grandfather had a block of about four to five acres of trees, which was a good-sized home orchard.

My father started delivering apples into LaPorte around 1915. There was a cider mill in LaPorte, on Jay Street, and he took apples up there to get them ground and pressed.

Then, in 1925, my father planted the first orchard of what we call modern times. He had about twelve acres to start with. Then, in the fifties, there were probably twenty-five acres. My three brothers and I formed a partnership and bought the ground from my father, this farm here.

If you're talking about grain farmers, we sound like nothing, because this farm's about 325 acres. But an acre of fruits and vegetables compares to ten acres of grain farm as far as input and output. That's probably changed a lot with six-, seven-dollar corn.

And the economy has changed in that

> *"Adolescent trees in general have more skin problems. They're sort of like people. I'm not joking."*

people don't buy stuff for home freezing and canning the way they used to. They'd buy bushels of broccoli, bushels of green beans, bushels of cauliflower. Those days are gone. Everybody buys a little bag of this or that for tomorrow. A lot of local people will come back to our market every week.

But Apple U-pick is still very popular, especially for city people. The Illinois trade is what makes it. You look at the parking lot out here on Saturday or Sunday, it'll be 75 percent Illinois plates. We used to sell twenty-pound drawstring bags of apples. Now people pick five pounds; it's just a walk in the orchard, something they can't do in Chicago.

Honey Crisp apples are the most popular thing going. They're very difficult to grow because it's an apple that'll look great coming up to harvest, and then you start getting speckles, spots on the skin. We do all kinds of special things to try and avoid that. We put calcium sprays on probably seven times because that's the main theory: that they need a lot of calcium and the only way you can get enough calcium in them is to put it on the leaf. It wouldn't do any good to put it on the ground because it wouldn't absorb fast enough.

Adolescent trees in general have more skin problems. They're sort of like people. I'm not joking. You try to get a smooth skin on a Golden Delicious on a real young tree and it's very, very difficult. They want to get a little russet on them. We do a lot of things to prevent it, but it's part of growing up and getting through a certain stage with their life.

We're right on the edge of the prairie country and the hill country here. Hills are the best place for an apple orchard. You don't want an apple orchard on low ground because the frost in the spring is on low ground and that's when you're trying to avoid getting hurt. You try to plant vegetables in the low parts. The frost isn't going to bother them because it's too warm by the time you get to vegetable season.

We get a lot of snow—that's partly the lake effect. In other words, you get a northwest wind and the air's moving across the water, it's picking up moisture. It usually doesn't fall out over in Chesterton as much until it gets about to this area, where it starts dumping between here and South Bend. Some people said that's due to the steel mills in Gary—they're putting so much carbon in the air and so forth. Well, the steel mills went out of business for all practical purposes. We still get snow.

SCOTT TUCKER

MAPLE LEAF FARMS

People are often surprised to learn that Indiana produces and exports more duck than any other state. There's a good chance that if you order duck in any restaurant in the United States, that bird's a Hoosier. Maple Leaf Farms has been at the forefront of this growth industry. Accounting for about 50 percent of duck production in the United States, Maple Leaf has focused on the white-tablecloth food service trade, as well as retail markets. "We've made a real point of trying to make duck available for people in a restaurant setting where it's going to be prepared appropriately, where they're going to get the right first impression," says Scott Tucker who, with his brother John, serves as co-president of the business. We met Scott at Maple Leaf's newly expanded headquarters in Leesburg, the base from which Maple Leaf Farms is developing a worldwide reach.

{Leesburg}

Big duck on a small pond

My grandfather, Donald Wentzel, is a native of northern Indiana. Back in the forties, he was a feed salesman for an organization in Chicago that sold feed to Long Island duck producers. At that time, I believe there were three of them out there raising ducks on expensive real estate, having to truck feed ingredients from the Midwest, where we are, all the way out to the East Coast. He just really didn't believe that was a long-term, viable business model.

He was let go from his seed-selling position, moved back to northern Indiana, and never forgot that duck experience. Started growing a few ducks on his own, having them processed on a contract basis. In 1958, there was a little processing plant up the road here in Milford, Indiana, that came up for sale, which he jumped on very quickly. Maple Leaf Farms was born. It's a true entrepreneurial story.

We've always had a philosophy here of if you're treating the animal well, if you're giving it the types of nutrients it needs, giving it the right types of shelter, and water at all times, that you're going to

"There are so many choices we have. And that's the blessing, the abundance of being in agriculture."

have not only a wonderful product that has good quality, but something that people will look at and say, "That's reasonable for me to eat."

It's so flavorful. It's versatile. People, for years, have just thought of roast duck a *l'orange*, the traditional French preparation. But duck can be prepared in as many ways as any other protein. It probably has a comparable fat content to chicken. Most people don't realize most of the fat is contained in the skin and the fat layer and, when that's removed, they're very comparable—although I tend to like to eat the skin. That's where all the flavor comes from.

There are so many choices we have, and that's the blessing, the abundance of being in agriculture. People have that luxury of looking deeper into it. I think at the end of the day, if you're trying to do the right things and providing a food source, people will come flocking to your door.

We are about 50 percent of the market share in the United States and throughout North America, with about twenty-six million ducks being produced annually. That gives you a sense of the actual numbers. It's nowhere near what the chicken industry does but, as I like to say, we're a big duck on a small pond.

But when you look at what we're doing in North America, it really pales in comparison to what goes on in the rest of the world. Europe probably produces ten times that many ducks. In China alone, they consume three and a half billion ducks annually. So while people in North America consider duck to be almost an afterthought, it's a mainstream protein in the rest of the world and a main part of their diets.

While we'll continue to try and grow duck here, and, hopefully, people will make that a part of their diets in the long term, we have a lot of opportunities in those areas where we know they already eat duck. That's where a lot of our attention is focused.

In China, for instance, only about 20 percent of the ducks produced there are done on a commercial basis, which means done in a more controlled, food-safe, environment. And that's one of the advantages we bring through our system. We like to call it the INDUX system, where we help a producer in a commercial setting by not only bringing them breeding stock, but the type of feed rations, the type of husbandry practices, to ensure safety. All told, that produces a much safer, more efficient animal, which—as much as corn and soybeans cost today—that producer is not only looking for a safe product, but he's looking for ways to do that in an economical manner. That's the true advantage we bring after fifty-three years of being in business.

You know, some people, when I take them over to my home and prepare a duck breast on the grill, sometimes they'll compare it to steak, in terms of its quality and juiciness. But duck is its own flavor, not like chicken, where whatever sauce it's served with is what it tastes like. Duck has its own unique flavor profile without being the gamey, wild flavor somebody remembers from the one their grandfather shot.

MIKE HORRALL

MELON ACRES

You could call Highway 41 south of Terre Haute "melon miles." In this part of the state, the sandy soil provides an ideal bed for watermelons and cantaloupes, and during the summer and into the fall, you can buy them at numerous roadside stands and markets. The Horrall family has been farming 1,800 acres here since 1976 and selling their produce, which includes asparagus, sweet corn, and cucumbers, to grocery stores, restaurants, and plenty of motorists.

{ *Oaktown* }

Just like sugar

Most people think about watermelons in July and August—hot summer months. That helps us a lot. Our season coincides with when most people are eating watermelons: going to the beach, vacations, weekends.

They were growing watermelons in Oaktown in the horse-and-buggy days. There are old pictures of the railroads coming through and gentlemen out there with their horse and buggies full of watermelons, loading them on the railroads going to Chicago, St. Louis.

We're well known for cantaloupes as well. Most people that grow cantaloupe and watermelon in Knox County tend to it from the seedling all the way through. They make sure it gets what it needs so it's the best-tasting melon it can be. You've got to love it to do it because it's kind of a tough way of life. When it's time to pick them, you've got to pick them. You can't miss that opportunity. When they're ready, you've got to be dedicated to get out there and get them.

For years and years, it was seeded watermelons; now it's seedless watermelons.

"You've got to love it to do it because it's kind of a tough way of life."

And seedless are harder to grow than seeded because it's a triploid. It's not a hybrid, it's a triploid: a crop combination of three different plants.

From what I know about the growers in Florida and Georgia, most them are bigger and they probably contract a lot of their work out. They're not actually out in the fields as much as the Indiana guy. We walk our fields every day and look at the plants in the nursery and the greenhouses.

I love the challenges and the people I get to work with, the ones that come back every year to buy watermelons from us. You used to see a lot of what we call peddlers, somebody that would buy 100 watermelons and 100 cantaloupes and some sweet corn and sell it out of a pickup truck. You'd see them three or four times a week for a couple of months and get a relationship with them.

It's kind of nice to be able to sit down and forget about things and eat the best part of a watermelon. A peddler might want to see what one looks like. Or maybe there's a buyer or the inspector that comes every year from Kroger. Maybe it's a family member. We take ten minutes and cut a watermelon and enjoy it. The first few are especially good. Not getting to eat it, you forget how it tastes over the course of the winter.

I guess the perfect watermelon would be a somewhat long, oval shape. It would always have a good, yellow belly on it. That's what most people think of when they think of a ripe watermelon. They roll it over and look at the stomach. Now some of them don't have that belly on them like the older ones used to. But a nice yellow belly will tell you it's ready to pick. When you cut it, it tastes just like sugar.

JEAN KAUTT

BLOOMINGFOODS

Bloomingfoods consumer co-op got its start in a vacant two-story carriage house on Kirkwood Avenue in Bloomington. Over thirty-five years later, Bloomingfoods has three stores that are still owned by the people they serve. Based on a code of international principles, cooperatives are member-owned, member-governed businesses that operate for the benefit of their members. Jean Kautt, head of member services and outreach, has worked for Bloomingfoods for over thirteen years. "It's fantastic," she says, "to work for an organization that is so universally known, highly regarded for being credible, and supportive of health in every way you could think of."

{ *Bloomington* }

I want that

Our first storefront opened in July 1976. People in Bloomington came together to get hold of the kinds of food they wanted to eat and were not finding in the conventional grocery stores. The people who started Bloomingfoods really wanted a particular kind of food. They wanted organic. They wanted to be able to have a place where they could go and buy locally grown food. And they wanted

to be able to buy lots of different kinds of food in the bulk department so they could choose the size of package or bring their own packaging.

The amount of money that's tied up with our food dollars nationally in marketing and packaging, and the shipping of those packages, is huge. So you're being value conscious on numerous levels when you're shopping in a bulk department.

Price and access is an interesting conundrum. We're known for organic food—natural food in general—but, specifically, organic and local and fair trade.

The United States government has a certification program to become certified organic. It's incredibly tedious. Organic growers are put through the wringer in a way that conventional growers are not. The transition process from a conventional piece of cropland into organic is highly legislated and very, very meticulously documented. It's expensive to go through that process at any scale, size-wise.

When you're buying an organic product, at any store, you need to know that you're paying a real price for that food. If you're a small beef rancher (and we have a lot of them in this state) with 100 head of cattle, you are maintaining your business without government subsidy.

My favorite quote about price disparities and local food being elitist was from a blogger who said, "How is it elitist to buy food from someone with dirt under their fingernails?" If you had to pay for all the extra things in the store that are part of the bigger system, the price would be a lot different. In the co-op world, we've opted out of the big system. You've heard of people who've gone off the grid with regard to electricity and other modern conveniences and are doing their own thing to meet their needs. That's what we're doing. Co-ops exist to meet the needs of their members.

Some people still have the perception that co-ops are owned, run by, and shopped in by hippie types. They think that when I accept a speaking invitation I'll show up in tie-dye with dreadlocks. It's just not the case.

If you're in our stores now, you will see athletes galore. You will see senior citizens who look like they could be on a magazine cover because they're fitness and health models. You'll see families who are on WIC [U.S.D.A Women, Infants, and Children program] and use EBT [electronic benefit transfer] cards, which we accept. You will find people from the food pantries here in town where we've gone to teach how to shop in bulk and cook, so their dollars stretch further.

We have about 35 percent local produce in our stores; we're about 80 percent organic. If we could get it, we would be all local and organic. There are a lot of local farmers, though, who work at such a scale they sell everything they can through farmers' markets. They show up. They sell out. They don't have to deal with invoicing and deliveries. It's a simple, clean system, and it works great for them.

But we've found that, within a 100-mile radius around Bloomington, there are now about 300 different, meaningful-size family farms. They grow everything you could imagine wanting to eat, except for tropical fruit, coffee beans, and chocolate.

It's like a curtain is being pulled back from in front of the food industry. People are starting to ask why things are the way they are. There's an open-mindedness and a transparency, a lot of which has to do with social media. It's been a really good thing for our food system in general.

When our co-op reached the thirty-year mark we had about 4,500 members. In the past six years, we have come to almost 10,000. This is an indicator of how much awareness there is. Five years from now, the world of access to healthier kinds of foods is going to be even more different. People at all income levels are asking the questions: Where is it? How can I get that? I want that.

MARK SOUERS

IVANHOE'S

We walked into Ivanhoe's in Upland on a Wednesday afternoon. The place was packed. There was a line of teenagers waiting to place orders, and the dining room was full with people of all ages, enjoying Ivanhoe's sandwiches and, especially, its ice cream. Known for offering 100 different milk shake flavors, Ivanhoe's has been a fixture in Upland since 1965. Mark Souers has worked there since he was in high school.

{*Upland*}

All 100 flavors

Ivan and Carol Slain started Ivanhoe's. Ivan, at the time, was working over in Hartford City for Overhead Door, and he was thinking of going into business for himself. He drove by here one day—this used to be Wiley's Drive-In—and saw it was up for sale. Carol had been working as a teller at the bank here in Upland, so they decided to buy Wiley's Drive-In, and that's how they got started.

They had no idea that it would take off like it has. I've had people come in here from Minnesota and say that they heard about Ivanhoe's on the radio. Somebody had been to Ivanhoe's, and here they are on this national radio station talking about us. These people hear about it, they're driving through Indiana, so they stop. Who would have ever thought that would happen?

Carol and Ivan used to close in the wintertime and go to Florida. Every year, Carol would try to think up some new creations, different combinations of ingredients for the shakes. She'd add four or five every year until all of a sudden they reached 100 and were like, "Whoa! Maybe we better stop!"

Over the years, we've changed some, taken the slow-movers off. But when you

work here, you get tired of eating the same thing, so you try to come up with something new.

The kids here come up with new creations. We also have seasonal items. In the fall, pumpkin shakes are real popular, though mint chocolate chip is most popular of all. The way we go through them is just unreal.

The weirdest thing I ever ran across was when I had a guy come in and say, "I hear I can get whatever I want?" I said, "Whatever we have, we'll do it for you." And he said he wanted a cookie dough shake with French fries added to it. So I cooked him up a few fries and threw them in his cookie dough shake. I didn't try it. I think he was just testing us.

There was a Taylor University student that tried all 100 flavors. He came in on his 100th one, and his friends threw him a little party. A couple months later, he sent us a picture from it along with a plaque his friends made with his name on it, and he said, "You guys should start a 100 Club." So we did it; we have a 100 Club. There's a card and we stamp it, and when you get done, we give you a T-shirt that says you completed Ivanhoe's 100 Club, and your name goes on that plaque.

A couple of years ago, the whole freshman class at Taylor completed it. We made 100 shakes, took them down to homecoming, and they had 100 students line up and try all 100 shakes at one time. That was impressive: to see 100 shakes on a table.

We have three sizes of shakes: the mini, a regular, and then we have the super. Before I worked here, when I was fourteen or fifteen, I came in and I thought I was going to be a big person and I got a super shake. That is a quart of ice cream. Now I know what a super is, so I don't think I ate the whole thing—at least not in one sitting.

I think it was chocolate chip. My wife says I'm boring. I like the simple ones.

One of the other managers (he's still here) knew my parents, and he told them that when your son gets sixteen, you have him come down to Ivanhoe's and get a job. I came in, but I didn't think I would still be here. Actually, I worked my first night, my second night, and I didn't want to come back. I was so shy—and you deal with a lot of people.

My parents encouraged me, and I did come back. Now I'm the PR guy at Ivanhoe's. I love being involved in the community, so I enjoy it.

My wife works here with me, and she said she had a couple of ladies stop here and say everything was great, how good it was, and complimented us. They said so many restaurants are changing things, trying to go cheaper, and they said, "Please, don't change nothing!"

GARY MORRIS

CLABBER GIRL CORPORATION

We met Gary Morris, the president and chief operating officer of one of Indiana's most venerable brands, Clabber Girl Baking Powder, in the handsome, turn-of-the-century office building created by Herman Hulman, one of the founding brothers behind Hulman & Company, the wholesale grocery and manufacturing business started in Terre Haute in 1850. Today, the Clabber Girl brand is sold throughout the United States and in many countries around the world. Clabber Girl Corporation distributes retail, wholesale, and industrial size baking powder under a variety of different names. The ground floor of Clabber Girl's headquarters has been turned into a museum, coffee shop, café, and kitchen, where cooking classes are offered.

{ *Terre Haute* }

Connected to their roots

This business, Hulman & Company, which is the parent company of Clabber Girl, is 161 years old and still owned by the same family, the Hulman family, that started the business in 1850. In today's world, that, to me, is an amazing, amazing accomplishment.

You hear a lot about corporations and how they're just out to be greedy. Obviously, you have to be successful to be profitable, but the Hulman family and the board of directors has been supportive of this business. They're completely vested in the growth and development of the organization. They're connected to their roots.

This building we're in was built in 1892. The Hulman brothers started the business in 1850. So Herman Hulman was probably in his late sixties, early seventies when he built this building. Look around at this structure. I mean, this is quite an undertaking for somebody that age, who'd already been in business forty years.

He built the business up in the middle seventies of that century. Started making baking powder. At the same time, they were making all kinds of food items. They were canning vegetables, roasting coffee, which, Rex Coffee, we still do today. Making peanut butter.

Herman had one son, and that was Anton Hulman, Sr., and Anton had one son,

"And the reference became, you know, 'Get the Clabber, the one with the girl.'"

Tony Hulman, Jr. Tony was the fellow who took Clabber Girl Baking Powder in the early twenties and made it a nationally distributed product. Back in the early twenties you could go across the United States, and there were baking powder companies in every single area. There was no national distribution network to get the product out. So there were literally hundreds and hundreds of local folks making baking powder. We're still here because of what Tony Hulman, Jr., did in making this a nationally distributed product.

Clabber refers to clabbered, or soured, milk. They would use sodium bicarb[onate] and then ash from the fire, with acid milk, or soured milk. And the acid would interact with the soda and release gas. But this would vary because the acid content was never the same.

About the 1890s, a girl showed up on the can. And the reference became, you know, "Get the Clabber, the one with the girl." In 1922, they patented the formula and registered the trademark as Clabber Girl. It went forward across the country as Clabber Girl Baking Powder.

Today we have Clabber Girl Baking Powder, Rumford Baking Powder. We also produce Royal Baking Powder, which is very popular out West for Hispanic populations. Davis Baking Powder's the number one baking powder on the East Coast. We do private label.

Clabber Girl has been around since people were growing their own produce and making their own bread. That hasn't changed. We think if you prepare your own food and you know where your materials come from, you make it healthy. That's why we teach cooking classes.

We have summer camps for kids where they come in half days for various age groups. We teach them how to cook because that is something that is lost today. Nobody cooks from scratch at home. So who's teaching these kids how to do it? We bring them into the classroom here, and they're so proud when they make things and bring them home to their mom and dad.

On weekends, during the farmers' market, there's always some kind of class going on in here using products from across the street that aren't necessarily related to baking, just cooking from scratch. We have chefs that will come in and do various ethnic cooking classes.

What's great is to go through the archives and see Herman Hulman's notes—his name or his initials, where he's written or signed for something or written a note to somebody. Tony Hulman, Jr., the same way, with all his personal notes.

Our vision is to make this business sustainable so that the next generation can do what we're doing or have the same opportunities, so we're part of something a lot bigger than ourselves.

DANIEL ORR
FARMBLOOMINGTON

When Chef Daniel Orr opened FARMbloomington restaurant just off the town square in the picturesque town that's home to Indiana University, he found a happy medium that, in a sense, summed up his culinary career. Orr is an Indiana native who's headed kitchens in places as diverse as Manhattan and the Caribbean island of Anguilla. As he tells it: "Both islands are about thirteen miles long and two or three miles wide. But in Manhattan and the five boroughs, you have twelve million people and Anguilla had 12,000 people. When I came back to Indiana, I decided that it felt like somewhere in between Anguilla and New York. Driving around, you could be in the country in five minutes. I could raise my own produce; I could know my farmers and look them in the eyes."

{Bloomington}

Exciting, seasonal, fresh

I've been around the world. I've known a lot of people from other countries who've taught me to cook their dishes. So I try to bring some of those spices and some of those ingredients in and then use local ingredients as much as possible. It's local food with global influences.

When I think of Midwestern food, I think of my grandmother's kitchen—country cooking of the early 1900s. I go back and I look at some of these old cookbooks—I collect old cookbooks—and see what people were doing then and kind of add my own twist.

We do southern fried chicken every Wednesday night. We do meatloaf every Tuesday night. We do brisket on Thursday, and we do a firehouse catfish fry on Fridays. These are real Midwestern comfort foods. Our menu may be a little more eclectic, but we try to always have that underlying feeling of home cooking, things that people used to eat.

One of the things I do is forage. I go out and pick a lot of wild foods. I get cattail pollen and make cattail pollen muffins and pancakes. I've just brought in a bunch of elderberries, which I had to fight the

birds for, because they love them, too. So I made about four gallons of elderberry syrup that we can use on our local peaches; we can make elderberry vinegar and deglaze pans with pork chops. I pick the elder flowers in the spring and we make a sweet tempura; we fry them and they're crispy, very lacy looking. I get chanterelles in early July—last year I probably picked fifty pounds of chanterelles. I get wild greens, lamb's quarter, mustard, onions, ramps (which are the wild leeks). Every season there's something to pick from the wild harvest.

"We don't do things that are stacked up or artsy-fartsy. We want food to speak for itself."

We'll do a lot of processing of wild ingredients and local garden harvests. We make all kinds of flavored salts. When we've got fresh herbs, we'll make purple basil salt, we'll make sage garlic salt, we'll make rosemary salt with these things that are coming from my garden or from local farmers. We'll make dried tomatoes, tomato sauces.

We use local meats. We get Fiedler Farms beef and pork and Glick Brothers grass-fed beef; our chickens and pork also come from Gunthorp Farms—we get rabbits from them. We get local eggs from Luke Rhodes, who also brings us duck eggs, whenever they're available.

In the winter, of course, we can cold-storage things like sweet potatoes, cabbages, and all kinds of squash and be using them pretty much through the next spring. We use Burton's Maple Syrup from Burton's Maplewood Farm, and local honeys.

There are people who want their strawberries, even in December, which doesn't really make sense. But in a college town, you've got to give people what they want and make them happy. I think we find a nice balance of buying things less expensively from bigger vendors and then using the little farmers, as well. I think we balance it out so the prices aren't too expensive. They're not cheap, but we try to have something for everyone.

Every day I do a small-plates menu, which is eight to ten different things that are just available that day. There may be five of one, there may be seven of another, there may be fifteen of another item. You have to get here at five o'clock if you want to have the whole choice, because, by the end of the night, we try to sell out of all those dishes. I try to use small amounts of things. Let's say we get a beautiful bunch of radishes. We'll turn that into a salad with local cucumbers and tomatoes and fresh herbs. It's exciting, it's seasonal, it's fresh.

I opened my restaurant at the very worst time in the economy, but we're doing well; we're expanding. I have a clientele that is very loyal. They come in a lot. There're certain people that eat almost every dinner here—they're wealthy young couples and they don't have kids; they just like to come to dinner. Then there are lots of people that come two or three times a week. We have to be on the ball and keep our game up because there are people who drive from farther distances. We have people from Chicago who come down and want to eat here. They say they can't find anything like this in Chicago, which is hard for me to believe.

But I think we try to hit a certain simplicity in our cuisine and presentation. We don't do things that are stacked up or artsy-fartsy. We want food to speak for itself. I say that being a great chef is 90 percent being a good shopper and 10 percent not messing up what you bought. That's my philosophy.

FAMILY

"A family business is tough sometimes, but we get over our differences, and we don't hold grudges."

CAROL SHOUP

THE RESLER GENERATIONS

BLUE-RIBBON COMPETITORS

Fancheon Resler, her daughter Kenda Resler-Friend, and granddaughter Klaine Friend represent three generations of enthusiasm for the Indiana State Fair. Since 1948, when Resler made her first entry in one of the fair's many food competitions, she and her offspring have filled a good-sized wall with blue ribbons, and have made the annual statewide gathering a family tradition. Resler-Friend goes so far as to keep her lifetime pass to the fair in a locked safe. "I'm going to get about sixty years out of this pass," she says happily.

{ *Albion and Indianapolis* }

My best recipe

Kenda: The Indiana State Fair takes me back to my roots. It takes me back to summers in the kitchen with Mom, putting our entries together. It's something Mom and I do together, which I am blessed to be able to do. We almost feel like the fair is ours, like we're ambassadors. We'll tell you how to find the bathroom or the best ice cream. We have many state fair ties. Klaine, how old were you when you first went to the state fair?

Klaine: Oh, under one.

Kenda: You were three weeks old.

Fancheon: I remember changing her diaper down in Culinary Arts.

Kenda: I've got pictures of Klaine at three weeks old going to the state fair. I mean that's all she knows in terms of the summer.

Fancheon: You don't have to be any age—just able to do it yourself. She's been doing it five years. What did you first enter?

Klaine: Nonbaked cookies. Peanut butter balls.

Fancheon: And how did your rolls compare to your grandma's for the first two or three years? You beat me every time!

Klaine: I beat her.

Fancheon: If we go way back, probably when I was eleven, my canned beets came to the state fair. The next year, it was my canned peaches.

Kenda: So your beets came before you did.

Fancheon: Yes. The county agent brought them. But I got a blue ribbon at the state fair.

Kenda: So you were in 4-H and I was in 4-H. And this is Klaine's first year in 4-H.

Fancheon: We lived in the country and in the summertime, basically, other than

"She sometimes even brings her refrigerator."

church and Sunday school, 4-H was the only time I was with other kids, other than my own brothers and sisters. Going to the club meetings was fun.

Kenda: I was at State Fair Youth School. It's kids from all over the state that come together. Back then you stayed at the fair. You were there before it opened to help set up and get ready.

Fancheon: You stayed in those old buildings that have now been remodeled.

Kenda: I won scholarships because of different things in 4-H. And I won that pony. Then I won a horse from Bob Evans. That's a whole other story.

Fancheon: I wanted to know how to compete, so I took judging classes and I became a judge. Then I found a recipe called Mexican Cornbread. It was just a loaf, but it was wonderful. I took the recipe and made it into a double braid. But, in the first years, when I called it Mexican Cornbread, nah, I'd get a first prize, but that was it. Then I called it Confetti Fiesta Braid, because I had six colors of peppers and cheddar cheese and cream-style corn, and I won the national award!

Kenda: So the name—there's something in a name.

Fancheon: There really is. You learn all these things competing. It is a very tasty bread. It's not my best bread recipe; it is my best recipe.

Kenda: It's why my husband married me.

Fancheon: Oh, that's right!

Klaine: No, no. That was for cinnamon rolls.

Fancheon: This is really funny: The first time Kenda brought [her husband] Brian home, she said, "He wants rolls." I thought she said he wanted rules. And I made ten rules for Brian before he arrived!

Kenda: It's amazing he still married me!

Fancheon: Oh, goodness, yes. We just have a lot of fun. It's just so neat for me to be able to reserve that time in August because I do so much volunteer stuff. I give away lots and lots of food. I give away a lot of practice food. I mean, for me, that's kind of a mission. You're always trying something new. You know what, Klaine? This year I'm doing red velvet cheesecake bars.

Klaine: I already called cheesecake.

Fancheon: Well, but yours will be different.

Kenda: Grandma comes and stays with us during the state fair.

Klaine: It's like Thanksgiving!

Fancheon: And what does Grandma bring with her? She sometimes even brings her refrigerator. Certainly the mixer.

Kenda: The mixer you gave me for my wedding must not have been good enough.

Fancheon: It's not! It's not my Bosch with the good dough hooks.

Kenda: It's just fun. We don't get too worked up.

Klaine: Not *too* worked up.

Kenda: Klaine, what do you say, babe? Are you competitive?

Klaine: Yes.

Fancheon: She really likes to beat us!

HEATHER HILL

HILL FARMS

Hill Farms, located in Greenfield, was started by Steve and Debbie Hill in 1973. Hill Farms is known for its pigs—it sends about 13,000 hogs to market every year—but the Hills also grow corn, soybeans, and wheat on 1,300 acres of cropland. Heather Hill is Steve and Debbie's daughter-in-law. Heather was elected president of the Indiana Pork Board in 2012. She calls the birth-to-market process of farming livestock a way of life. "We know that's part of the life cycle, what the animals are here for us to do, and we just enjoy being able to be a part of that."

{ Greenfield }

We put our all into it

My husband is the next generation of Hill Family Farms, so a fourth-generation farmer. We have been married twelve years; I kind of married into the family farm. My mom grew up on a pig farm. I grew up in 4-H, showing livestock. I was an animal-science major at Purdue. Though I didn't actually grow up on the farm, agriculture was always near and dear to my heart. I consider myself very lucky that I was able to marry into such a great family farm.

We are a farrow-to-finish operation, which means we have the sows that give birth to the pigs here, then we leave our pigs on the mother sow for about three weeks so they can nurse. At about three weeks of age, we wean them and move them to what we call a nursery room. They are there from three to ten weeks, and we move them again to what we call a finisher, which is a group pen where, depending on the size of the room, there might be 200 pigs. They can move around and have access to feed and water.

Our pigs live on slotted cement floors. That way the manure and essentially all the waste can go down through the slats and into our pits. We have a very deep pit, kind of like a basement, underneath all our hog buildings. A couple times a

"Raising pigs is our livelihood, and we put our all into it each and every day."

year, we actually can suck the manure out through a hose system. We're able to put it into a tank with hoses and knives that we take to our fields. We knife the manure into the fields as an organic fertilizer. It drastically reduces, if not eliminates, our need for man-made fertilizers. I call the pig the ultimate recycler because we use their manure to fertilize the field to grow the corn to feed them.

Our pigs eat a corn-based diet, which, for the most part, is raised by us. We mix all the feed here at our own feed mill. It's a constant battle: making feed, delivering the feed to the feed bin so the pigs can get it, checking their waters, making sure the pigs are healthy, keeping up-to-date records.

Six months would probably be the average life cycle for a market pig. Basically, we're constantly monitoring them to make sure they're healthy, that they're growing correctly. When they reach that target weight of about 280 pounds, we have a truck driver that we work with who comes and we'll do a semiload of pigs. We don't sell a semiload every week, but my husband sold two semiloads on Sunday. He's selling two today. We sell the majority of our pigs to Tyson, which has a processing plant in Logansport, Indiana.

Local seems to be a popular word in terms of "we want local foods." I think we really need to think about what local means. A lot of the pork that ends up in the grocery stores in Indiana probably has a very good chance that it came from pigs in Indiana. I bought some pork chops at Walmart, and, when you flip them over, they say distributed by Tyson Foods. I like to think perhaps those came from our pigs—or, at least, one of the pig farmers I know in Indiana.

I am proud to be one of Indiana's family pork farmers. Ninety-four percent of the pork farms in Indiana are family-owned. We're not the biggest of the big, but we're not the smallest of the small. But even the big family farmers, they're still families.

I just want people to know that, truthfully, we start out each and every day providing the best care to our pigs. The decisions we make are because we have done a lot research, we've put a lot of time into it, and we've been doing it for generations. We know what works, what doesn't work, and we're also willing to try new things because we can't go back and live fifty years ago. If we all want to survive, we have to continue growing. And I just want people to know that raising pigs is our livelihood, and we put our all into it each and every day.

LOIS RUST AND RUTH ANN HENDRIX

ROSE ACRE FARMS

Rose Acre Farms is the second-largest egg producer in the United States, with literally millions of chickens laying eggs at its various facilities in five states for brands such as Eggland's Best. We met Rose Acre's matriarch, Lois Rust, and her daughter, Ruth Ann Hendrix, where the Rose Acre story begins, on the outskirts of Seymour. It's a story that, in many ways, outlines some of the ways American agriculture has evolved since the middle years of the twentieth century.

{Seymour}

Never a dull minute

Lois: We've been here since 1954. There was an estate sale, and David, my husband, bought forty acres of it. This was west of Seymour and around old Highway 50.

My husband had a country egg route that he started from his family's home on a farm about four or five miles northeast of here. They took sweet corn to the south side market at Indianapolis. They would be up there at four o'clock in the morning, and the grocery stores came and stocked up from all the produce people there.

Finally, about 1943, when he was in high school, he would haul all the eggs he could in a car. He kept the egg route going because the sweet corn was seasonal.

By then, the grocery stores were changing. There was a grocery on about every fourth corner in Indianapolis. The first supermarkets were just starting. I know one used twenty cases of eggs a week, another used five cases, where, before, they would use maybe two cases or a case a week.

My husband continued at the south side market until about 1955. Then he started delivering to the stores. At first he was just using his parents' eggs. Then he would buy from aunts and uncles and neighbors.

There were several egg buyers out of

"If you turn a baby chick over in your hand, and then you rub its belly, it'll fall asleep."

Cincinnati. If they needed eggs, they would bid up and pay a high price. Well, one week my husband went around and there were no eggs. But we had to have eggs for our customers, so we decided that we had better start having some of our own. That's the only reason we ever got into layers.

It was different. We had to learn how to manage chickens. I grew up taking care of chickens and so did he. We knew the basics but to take care of them and grain them and do the whole thing, that took some management. If you do everything you're supposed to do, everything works fine. The main thing you don't want is for them to get sick. And new diseases come through every now and then, so a person has to always be on the lookout.

The chain stores started up, and we started servicing them. They grew; we grew. And basically, at one point in time, we decided that we either had to get larger or get out because they told us, "We need the eggs. If you can't supply us, we'll get someone else." That's the only reason we grew to the size we did. There was never a dull minute.

Ruth Ann: It's fun, but you grow up with it, so it's your normal.

I studied at IU Bloomington. I got over there and studied a lot of nineteenth-century things, and I was like, well, that's what it's still like at home!

I like producing food. We all eat every day. And eggs are a good source of protein, one of the cheapest proteins. During hard economic times, people tend to trade down their protein values, so eggs do well even when the economy's not so strong.

I love chickens, too. If you turn a baby chick over in your hand, and then you rub its belly, it'll fall asleep. It's fun to watch their eyes close.

The other thing about chickens: They like to feel taken care of. If you are carrying them, as long as you make sure both their wings are close to something, they don't panic. You don't want a chicken panicked. A lot of ours grow up in cages, and so that's their normal. When they get out, they're just like, oh, what's going on? Then they run, and it's hard to catch them. I had to catch a lot of chickens; their hearts are racing. Then you get them back in their cage, and they're good again.

BILL OLIVER

OLIVER WINERY

When Bill Oliver's father, Indiana University law professor William Oliver, helped pass legislation allowing for the creation of small wineries in 1971, many people scoffed at the idea of Indiana becoming associated with viticulture. But now there are over sixty wineries operating throughout the state, attracting almost one million visitors a year. As for Oliver Winery, its annual sales have topped 270,000 cases, and its Creekbend label has been producing wines from Indiana-grown grapes at Oliver's Bloomington vineyard since 1994. "My dad started this whole thing," says Bill Oliver today. "I don't know if I would have had the courage to have initiated this. It's that entrepreneurship, where the first generation starts and the second generation builds it."

{*Bloomington*}

Full fruit in the glass

Dad moved to Bloomington in '59 and started growing grapes in '65 on a hobby basis. He started the winery in '72. It was a little hobby winery for maybe fifteen years until I showed up in '83 with a business degree and said, "Let's see what we can do with this thing."

I'd been to California and seen what they do out there and thought, really, there is no secret to it! A focus on the wine quality, but also the experience of visiting the winery, people coming in the front door, and people greeting them with a smile, some flowers out front—that kind of thing. Good quality wine and a pretty bottle, a pretty place, and nice staff: That's what we've focused on. It's really worked well for us.

Our objective is to get full fruit in the glass. What does it taste like? We can do some lab chemistry; check the sugars, pH, acidity. But what it really boils down to is: Do you like the way it tastes?

The biggest fear we face is a tropical storm remnant coming up from the Gulf. Like a hurricane hits New Orleans. By the time it gets here, it's just a big bunch of rain. Thirty-six hours of nonstop precipitation, which we get every third or fourth year. And these varieties of grapes are so ripe,

> *"Good quality wine and a pretty bottle, a pretty place, and nice staff:*
> *That's what we've focused on."*

so ready to rot if they get wet. So we're looking at the ten-day weather forecast, we're checking the grape maturity. It's a lot of hand wringing and second guessing and nervousness, you know, but it's all fun. It's good stuff.

I love to get the wine skeptics out here. Just me and a handful of them. We start at the beginning and talk about grape growing, why this is a great place. We taste the wine and, like, wow! We really do know what we're doing!

We have this guesthouse, and I'll get people out here, especially if they write a blog post or something that's uninformed. I write back, "Hey! Really want you to come down. Really want to spend some time with you." And almost every time, it's a complete 180. They're like, "Okay, now I get it." I don't think you can accomplish that just through advertising. We have to reach out to people and be patient and keep plugging away at it. It will never end.

I would say people today really like low acidity, they like big flavor, and they don't like a lot of tannins. That's that first impression of, "Do I like this glass of wine?" I'm thinking about what 95 percent of the people who drink wine think. That's my concern.

To develop those kinds of flavors and get that kind of acid profile, you need a place that's fairly warm. We talk about growing-degree days, which is a summation of heat throughout the year. It's what all farmers use, what agronomists use. It measures

warmth, in totality, over the season. We're about 3,500 growing-degree days here, exactly what Napa Valley is.

We're fortunate to be in south central Indiana, with our kind of heat summation, having the length of season we need to get grapes fully mature every year. I mean it's not some years; it's every year we get the kind of maturity we need.

Then we've got a really nice site. We've got well-drained soils on top of limestone. All soils on limestone are excellent. It's fractured; it's porous. Soils that are atop it are fairly well drained so we don't get extended periods of really wet soil, which is important for vine health.

Grape growing is my delight. In terms of what I enjoy sticking my nose into, it's the agricultural side, definitely. I wish I could drive tractors more. I've often said how the quality of my life is directly related to how much time I get to spend on a tractor. Way too much email, not enough tractors! I've got to work on that.

I remember standing on the front porch of that farmhouse over there and looking at soybeans and old fencerows and junk farm equipment going, "Someday this will be grapes!" I'm proud of all of us having the kind of patience to just plod along and get to this point. To think you plant a grape in the ground, a grape vine, which is a ten-inch stick with a few straggly roots on the bottom, and you think that some day you'll be making wine out of that … it's an act of, what should we say? Faith!

DARRELL AND CRAIG BROWN

BROWN FAMILY FARM

{ *Montpelier* }

Darrell and Craig Brown are father and son—and partners—on their eighty-acre farm in Montpelier, Indiana. Darrell is in his sixties and has a degree in agronomy from Purdue University. He spent the majority of his working life employed by the Soil Conservation Service, later the Natural Resources Conservation Service, an Indiana branch of the U.S. Department of Agriculture. He served as state agronomist for ten years. Craig grew up on the Montpelier farm and graduated from the University of Evansville with a degree in international studies. He and wife, Katie, returned to help start the Brown Family Farm after an extended sojourn in Oregon where they were involved with a CSA (community supported agriculture) farm. "I had the opportunity to travel around the state and see a wide variety of agriculture in Indiana," says Darrell as he and Craig sit under a shade tree on a windy afternoon. "Through those associations and Craig coming back to the farm, I guess I moved from a mainline traditional agriculture background to a sustainable one."

Living as they were made

Darrell: This was wild land. George Washington, when he was a young man, was a member of some of the parties that did the surveying.

At the north end of this eighty acres was where my grandmother grew up. There was a log cabin there that was long gone by the time I was born, but she told Dad that she had memories of seeing black bear walking along the little creek. So,

two generations back, it was still some pretty wild country.

Over here, about two miles, are the remnants of the Godfroy Reserve, which was an area that was given to Chief Godfroy through one of the treaties. It's all in private ownership now, but there was a ford there before there was a bridge, and Dad told of being a young boy, crossing the river at the ford, looking downstream and

seeing an encampment of Indians. This would have been in the 1930s.

When I was a kid, we were still a very diversified operation. We had hogs—farrow to finish—probably ten to fifteen sows; we probably had twelve to fifteen cattle. When my brother and I were in our early teens, Dad came home from work one day, and he said, "Boys, you're going to have to buy a ram." What for? Well, he'd bought ten

Columbia ewes that were trucked in here from Wyoming. The grasshoppers out there devoured everything, and there was nothing left to eat. So they shipped semiloads of those sheep east, and the stockyards over by Portland got truckloads and truckloads. Dad came home with ten of them at $10 apiece, so my brother and I bought us a ram, and we were in the sheep business.

Dad farmed this eighty acres—my grandfather was still living at that time—and then there was another eighty that he and my uncle farmed for my grandfather. In the early '60s, Dad bought another seventy-five acres across the road and then, in the early '70s, bought another eighty acres to the north of here.

As we got into the late '60s, early '70s, there was just a push nationwide for production. We were starting to develop worldwide markets, and it wasn't long until guys started to say, "Hey, maybe I don't want to mess with all the livestock."

Craig: Just get big or get out, right?

Darrell: Everybody thought they could be a big grain farmer like they are in western Indiana, northwest Indiana, northwest Ohio. Everybody thought it was bigger and better, so everybody had 80 or 120 acres, and the next thing you know, everybody that was trying to farm full-time was at 300 acres and then it was 500 acres …

Craig: Now it's what, 3,000?

Darrell: Yeah, 3,000 is kind of a starting point now. The '80s were really rough. Commodity prices were pretty good, but I paid 21 percent interest on operating money, and that was just horrible. I was a small operation farm, maybe 400 acres at the time, but I had to borrow and then pay 21 percent interest. There was a period of time in there when lots of people lost their farms. Inflation was bad.

Craig: This farm, as it exists now, would not be here without Mom and Dad. It's definitely a family affair. I guess we've just tried to keep it small and at a level that we can market everything that we sell via farmers' markets. I would not say that it's a living wage for either of us, at this point, but that's partly by choice. We eat really well and, to me, that is worth a whole lot. I've talked with other farmers and they feel the same way. The way we like to eat, we couldn't afford it if we weren't raising it. And so you have to add that to your asset column versus liability.

We've been trying to grow our beef herd for the past six or seven years, and it's still very small. When we started talking early on, the grass-fed component made a lot of sense to us from a nutritional standpoint. I think grass is what they're meant to eat. They have all those stomachs to convert grass to protein or milk. You can do it faster on grain, but there's a cost to be paid, both in terms of nutrition in the product and also for the nutrition of the animal.

To me, livestock that's 100 percent grass-fed trumps organic because you can be a certified organic livestock farmer and still feed your livestock grain, as long as it's certified organic grain, which always feels to me like they missed the memo. But it's a choice—and it's their choice to raise grain-fed livestock. To me, as a customer, if I had a choice between certified organic meat or 100 percent grass-fed, it would be a no-brainer, especially if I were buying directly from a farmer that I could talk to about how they raise, what they feed.

Darrell: The animals, as they're raised here, they're living as they were made to live.

MISAO AND CLARA KURAYAMA

SATUMA JAPANESE RESTAURANT

Chef Misao Kurayama and his wife, Clara, have been serving authentic Japanese cuisine at Satuma Japanese Restaurant in Columbus since 1996. It didn't take long for Japanese people—in town to work or consult with automotive manufacturing plants in Columbus—to adopt the place. Now Satuma's clientele includes diners from Indianapolis, Batesville, Bloomington, and even as far as Louisville, Kentucky. Chef Misao, or "Father" to his fans, creates traditional and original dishes with a characteristic emphasis on fresh ingredients. Clara told us their story.

{ *Columbus* }

Like family

When our youngest son was little, I didn't want him to call my husband Dad or Daddy. I wanted him to be called Father. So I would call him Father all the time to try to get our son to call him Father. And everybody, all the waitresses, started picking up on it. Everybody has a tough time saying his name anyway, so I said, "Oh, just call him Father."

It stuck.

Now we can't go anywhere, from Indianapolis south, where he is not known as Father. My niece's kids call him Uncle Father.

My husband worked for a shipping company in Japan that had a restaurant in [West] Lafayette named Heisei. He was one of the chefs they sent over to help open it. I was at Purdue at the time and I worked there. He asked me out for about a year and a half before I said yes.

We married and went back to Japan.

Then the company came to him and said the manager at Heisei in Lafayette was requesting we both go back to work with him. We talked about it and decided it was probably what we should do. He worked there maybe a year and

a half. One Saturday night he said, "You know, if we're ever going to have our own restaurant, we need to start looking."

A friend of ours in Chicago said, "There's a market in Columbus of Japanese people that has not been served." There was a Japanese restaurant here, but it was Chinese-owned, trying to do Japanese.

The next week, we came down and we looked at Columbus. At that time, the population of Japanese families was about 500. They work in the manufacturing sector here, car-parts companies.

"He wanted to go home, but he didn't want to leave. We were just like his family."

At first, people would come in and say, "Eew, sushi? Eew, raw fish? You don't have any rolls and honey butter?" In the evenings, we always give traditional Japanese *oshibori*. An *oshibori* is a wet towel, so the person can wash their hands and face. A lot of people in Japan are coming from the train. It's typical for them to get an *oshibori*. We'd hand it to people and they'd say, "What's that for? Did you expect me to take bath?" That's the kind of thing we would hear. Then they'd see the sushi, and it would be, "Where did you get that? From the local river?"

We've Americanized some things to get people introduced to sushi. Those are popular, and then people try things they were saying "Eew" about before.

For example, we have a Crazy Sarah roll with soy paper on the outside instead of the traditional nori paper. It's red tuna and white tuna, which are both raw, and deep-fried shrimp and cream cheese, drizzled with a spicy sauce. We had a group of Japanese people try it, and they said it was very good. So it worked for them, as well.

I remember we were going to open on a Friday night, but we weren't quite ready. There were still a few things we wanted to clean up and modernize, and we decided to put off opening until Sunday.

But a group of four Japanese businessmen came here after work, wanting dinner. We felt guilty because they'd come, thinking we'd be open. We were having chips and pizza. Well, that night, we fed them chips and pizza and Coke! They came back on Sunday.

When we opened, our first customers were like our brothers, sisters, aunts, uncles, cousins. People just in from Japan would call us from the airport and say, "We'll be there in half an hour." They'd been here before, or the company they were visiting would give them the number. We would stay open.

We have a lady who comes from a little town south of Salem [about sixty miles away]. She'll call and order sushi to go. She drives up, picks it up, and goes back. Last August, a Japanese guy that had been here four or five years was transferred to China. Instead of going home to Japan, he came here to see us.

There was this gentleman whose name was Jun. His time was up here and he was being sent back to Japan. We decided to decorate the room for him, and I went to Burger King to get a crown, so he could be the king. Instead of the BK symbol, I put *Satuma* on it. He sat in the middle of the room, and each one of the Japanese men told stories about him, sharing their memories. I remember walking in, and he was sitting here just crying and crying because he wanted to go home, but he didn't want to leave. We were just like his family.

COLT REICHART

RED GOLD

When you start getting close to the town of Elwood in north central Indiana, you're bound to begin seeing large semitrailer trucks emblazoned with the distinctive retro logo of Red Gold Tomato products. A four-generation family-owned business, Red Gold now employs 1,300 full-time workers and distributes its products nationwide and in fifteen other countries. Red Gold includes five major regional brands and private label brands for such retailers as Kroger and Walmart. "We probably do 90 percent of the private label ketchup alone," says Colt Reichart, great-grandson of founder Grover Hutcherson and director of Red Gold's new media initiative.

{ *Elwood* }

Meant to be here

I love tomatoes! The thing is, I probably eat them every day. I never get tired of them. Sometimes I'll have a jar of salsa just for dinner … and that will be it!

Growing up, you just didn't see your parents that much in the summertime. There were long hours, fourteen-hour plus days. They'd come home and they would smell funny. It wasn't from the fields; it was from the factory. It was a lot of concentrated tomatoes, tons and tons of them, just wicked into the fabric of their clothes.

Back in World War II, it seemed like every town had a tomato cannery because tomatoes were still handpicked, hand-cored, and hand-peeled, and transporting them very far with a tractor and a flatbed was impossible. It took a large labor force to do a seasonal job.

My great-grandfather owned and operated thirteen tomato canneries in his life. He was retired but felt forced back into the business after World War II started. He bought and rebuilt a burnt-out cannery and called it Orestes Canning Company. His daughter Fran, my grandmother, was already working with the family business when she married my grandfather, Ernie Reichart. Together, they bought the Red

"Indiana, right here where we are, has some of the best soil in the U.S."

Gold label from a packing company in Trafalgar, Indiana, that was going out of business.

They had three children—Brian, Gary, and Tina—and all three worked here. My dad, Brian, purchased Red Gold from my grandfather in the '80s and had about eight full-time employees when he became the CEO/president. He turned a seasonal operated Red Gold into a full-time year-round operation by bringing tomato concentrate from California on railcars so that we could produce some sort of tomato product during the winter months.

If you look at the latitude on a map, you'll see ours is the same as Italy. Some people will say Italian tomatoes are the best, but we have exactly the same climate and conditions.

Indiana, right here where we are, has some of the best soil in the U.S. The Tipton Glacier melted and ended right here, specifically Tipton County, our neighboring county, where many acres of Red Gold tomatoes are grown. All the minerals and topsoil scraped from the surface of our continent by this enormous glacier were deposited right here.

We've taken our hybrids and made different varieties: some that you plant early, some that you plant later in the year, some that are better for juice, and some that are better for peeling. We plant about 14,000 acres of tomatoes, 11,000 tomato plants per acre and each plant produces about ninety tomatoes.

Back in the day, tomatoes were hand-peeled and hand-cored. It's amazing today. You get more tomatoes per plant, they're coreless, they're firmer and they're stronger. There are twenty-three tons of tomatoes in a truck when they're delivered here, and the tomato on the bottom looks just like the tomato on the top. They don't get crushed! The tomatoes go through the canning process, so they're thick, like Romas. They are real meaty and they peel easier. You can actually lift a tomato plant off the ground, and if you shake it just once, every tomato will drop off. Another pretty neat thing about these hybrids is that most of them turn red at the same time.

People used to tout Indiana tomatoes, but that kind of disappeared. No one really talks about where tomatoes are from any more. I wish people knew, but some people are so picky. They want tomatoes from Italy or they want them from California. I don't know why they want them from there. I don't think they really know either. They've just been told that's where they're good.

It makes more sense to grow them here. Here, we have everything: sun, soil, rain. It's like tomatoes were meant to be here!

THE SHOUP FAMILY

SHOUP'S COUNTRY FOODS

Every Sunday, the extended Shoup family gathers for dinner. It's a family tradition that goes back generations. Today, mother Carol Shoup and her daughters Amy Shoup Mennen, Cindy Shoup Cacy, and Cheri Shoup Dayton preside over a thriving business in Frankfort that was started by Carol and her late husband, Tom. Shoup's Country Foods includes a retail meat store, a catering business that serves as many as 65,000 people in a year, and a mail-order branch that sends such original Shoup products as Mini-Hog Roasts and pork burgers, not to mention their trademark seasoning and BBQ sauce, to every state in the union. "It's what we would feed our family," says Carol of the Shoups' products. "It was important to Tom that we had the best that you could provide, at the best cost."

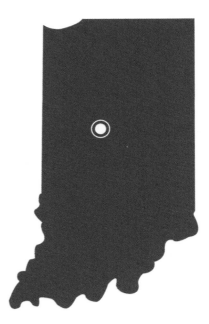

{*Frankfort*}

What we would feed our family

Carol: All I've ever known is cooking, and all the girls have known is cooking.

Cindy: I thought everyone had Sunday dinners with all their family. I really thought that was the norm.

Amy: It feels normal to us. Mom and Dad's siblings are all within a thirty-minute drive.

Carol: We've always had gardens, we've always canned, we've always frozen. We're just used to good food. We're kind of spoiled, I guess.

Amy: It's in our blood. My daughter's the same way. She just turned eleven and she can cook a whole meal. I'll come home, and she'll have a whole meal cooked! And my son likes to grill. Before it was the "in thing" for everybody to grill and barbeque, Dad was doing it with a makeshift grill and charcoal.

Cindy: Cooking is really an extension of our family because we show love to our family and our friends and neighbors through food. So when everyone gathers around a table for food, that's entertainment for us.

Amy: It makes you feel good. If there's a death or a marriage, you see the Shoup van come in …

"Dad invented the pork burger. That's not anywhere officially noted, but we're pretty sure."

Carol: A family business is tough sometimes, but we get over our differences, and we don't hold grudges.

Amy: Our dad invented the pork burger. That's not anywhere officially noted, but we're pretty sure. We've got records, even prior to the Indiana State Fair serving a pork burger. All these people thought they would cut all the good parts out of the hog and grind it up and season it and that was pork sausage. But Dad said, "Why do we always have to eat a good beef burger? Let's have a good pork burger."

Cindy: A pork burger is basically the same as what you would find in the very finest, extra lean, ground beef patty. So he took the same cuts and made a very good, extra lean, ground pork patty, that we call a pork burger.

Carol: It's not a by-product. It's a product.

Cindy: The other product we're kind of famous for is the Mini-Hog Roast. We have that trademarked. Everyone used to come into our place and they wanted to have a hog roast, but they didn't want to have 100 people over to the house.

Amy: The cool thing is it fits on any regular-size grill and feeds up to twenty-to-twenty-five people.

Carol: I guess my fondest memories are out in our yard, with a huge table, with all the little babies sitting around in high chairs with corn all over their faces. We had our own fried chicken, we had our own tomatoes, we raised everything in the meal: the peas, the lettuce.

Amy: I think that's a pretty good Indiana meal.

Carol: That's really satisfying.

Amy: Green bean sandwiches are one of our favorites. Grandma Shoup, on Dad's side, started the green bean sandwiches.

Cindy: I want one right now!

Amy: You've got to have fresh tomatoes and fresh green beans from the garden; the canned variety won't do.

Cindy: You cook the beans so they're tender—not al dente—then you drain them and you add bacon and onions. Then you put your bread down—and let's see if I do mine the same way you do—with your green beans and fresh garden tomatoes and a slice of onion with some mayo …

Amy: Hellmann's.

Cindy: And a little bit of salt and some Shoup seasoning. I'm telling you: We're meat eaters, but we could live on green bean sandwiches. We love them.

Amy: Sure. It's the best.

Carol: That is a Shoup tradition.

BRENT JOSEPH

KING DAVID DOGS

There's no mistaking a King David hot dog. It's a vivid shade of red, thanks to a recipe combining a unique mix of spices and a smoking process with a quarter pound of beef. "When you see hot dogs on the market and they're kind of a tannish color, that's because they're made with chicken and pork and turkey parts," says King David's owner, Brent Joseph. "There's not much beef to them." Brent resurrected his family's King David brand, based on his family's original hot dog recipe, when he opened a restaurant in a narrow storefront located in the heart of downtown Indianapolis. The rest is hot dog history. King David Dogs has become a popular destination for anyone with a craving for this iconic American food.

{ Indianapolis }

It's a hot dog place

I think a hot dog is kind of a universal food, one of those things people grew up with and have fond memories of. They start eating them when they're kids. Most families serve their kids hot dogs. They're easy to eat. They're easy to cook. They're easy to hold, and everybody can dress them up the way they want.

I tell people hot dogs are kind of like pizza. Everybody likes something different on their pizza. Same thing with a hot dog. There are people who like it plain. There are people that want only mustard. There are people who want ketchup. And there are people who say it's an absolute travesty to put ketchup on a hot dog. I say, to each their own.

The King David hot dog was created by my grandfather, William Hene, and his brother, my great uncle, Paul Hene, in the early forties after they immigrated to this country from Germany. My grandfather was an attorney in Germany and my great uncle Paul was a butcher. They escaped the Holocaust and the Nazis in Germany and settled in Indianapolis.

They were trying to figure out what to do. My grandfather's legal degree didn't transfer to the United States. So they had the idea of starting a meat company.

The Hene Meat Company was a large-scale, commercial butcher shop. It provided steaks, ground beef, summer sausages, beef bologna, liverwurst to local grocery stores, some smaller butcher shops, some restaurants, as well as catering companies and cafeterias. Out of all those products, the most popular was the all-beef hot dog.

My grandfather was killed in a car accident in '82. My great uncle Paul continued to run the business until he was in

> *"Make it a hot dog lover's utopia where, if you could think of it,*
> *we put it on a hot dog for you."*

his early nineties and couldn't do it anymore. Then they shut the doors and the brand went away.

I grew up running around the meat company when I was little. I have fond memories of seeing my grandfather and my great uncle in their white butcher coats and [of] the distinct smell of the smokehouse and going down there and having lunch and having hot dogs. Something I always regretted was not being able to be part of the family business. And, over time, we would hear, "Why can't we get King David hot dogs?"

I worked for a couple of different companies and did some different things. Wasn't doing anything that I was particularly thrilled with or wanted to do the rest of my life. One night I was sitting around on the couch with my wife, Hannah. We were having a couple of drinks, just trying to figure out what we wanted to do with our future. She said, "Why don't you bring the hot dogs back?"

Now, anybody can open up a restaurant and serve hot dogs. But our unique advantage was we had a hot dog that was exclusive to us. We had a product and a brand that had history to it. It is local. It was created in Indianapolis. And, frankly, it's better than almost anything you can find on the market.

Most hot dogs nowadays are more a vehicle for the condiments, the toppings you put on. It's basically more texture than taste and flavor.

Our hot dog is an all-beef, quarter-pound, skinless hot dog that is made exclusively for us. It is our own original family recipe and it's got some uniqueness and character to it that not many other products on the market have. There is more garlic in it than in most hot dogs. There's some pepper in it as well. The smoking process is part of it. And, again, it is an all-beef product. When I say all-beef, in the hot dog world that could mean a lot of different things. Our product is not only all-beef, it's all meat.

Both William and Paul's wives were still alive. We got blessings from them and the rest of the family to go ahead and see what we could do. Then we had to locate the recipe.

We went digging through my great aunt's attic and found a notebook squirreled away in a box that had the recipe for the hot dogs. It was in German. So we had to have it translated. My great aunt and grandmother got it. A professor took a look at it for us. Most of it was measurements for the meat mix and the spice mix.

The concept behind the restaurant was to call it King David Dogs and basically serve the best hot dog in town. Make it a hot dog lover's utopia where, if you could think of it, we put it on a hot dog for you. We've got thirty-plus toppings, everything from four kinds of cheese to four kinds of mustard to chicken chili to fried egg. We've tried peanut butter; we've tried mac and cheese.

We get the question, "Why don't you serve salad?" To be honest with you, if we were to do a salad, it probably wouldn't be that great. Do you really want to come and have a mediocre salad? You want to come to a hot dog joint and have a hot dog. We don't want to try and be something we're not. We don't want to detract from the feature of the menu and the restaurant. It's a hot dog place. We want to be the best at what we are.

BACK TO ROOTS

"And so we're all connected through time, through that place and through that food."

DANI TIPPMANN

DANI TIPPMANN
MIAMI TRIBE

"Our food is so much a part of our lives. It's just incredible," says Dani Tippman a member of the Miami tribe. Tippmann has been part of a Miami cultural resurgence in Indiana. She has served as an artist-in-residence at the Eiteljorg Museum of American Indians and Western Art in Indianapolis, doing workshops on Indiana plants and helping to plant a "Three Sisters Garden" of Miami corn, squash, and beans. Dani is also working on a Miami cookbook and is active in the preservation of the Miami language. We met her in Columbia City, where she is director of the Whitley County Historical Museum.

{*Arcola*}

Bones of our grandfathers

The Miami are traditionally from this area. We think we came out of the St. Joseph River, up by South Bend. That's an origin story. So this is where we've always been.

A lot of our traditional stories deal with food. This was an area where there were swamplands and woodlands. We were hunters and gatherers and gardeners. We had traditional garden foods—corn and beans and squash—and we also had the wild plants, like cattails.

Precontact, Miamis had their farms along what we call the shoulders of the river, the overflow area. When you think about that, it makes so much sense because, in the spring, the waters would overflow and kill the vegetation that's there. Then they would dry up and leave the silt, the new earth.

In General Anthony Wayne's journal, he talks about over 200 acres under cultivation of the finest corn and beans he has ever seen. So it amazes me that people don't consider the Miami as farmers; all they know are the warrior stories.

Our stories tell us that before corn, there were famines. After corn, there was not a recorded famine. It tells you that we were good farmers and that we depended upon

"And so we're all connected through time, through that place and through that food."

it. It made us a healthier community after we had corn and beans and squash. The way they act together in your body, it's a perfect mixture. It feeds you totally.

We have something called a Miami Rabbit Bean, because it looks like those "little beans" the rabbits leave in your yard. That one's been passed down. There's a squash that's been passed down. Then, of course, the white corn.

Our traditional white corn has been passed down through the generations from mother to daughter. It was very important to our culture. It was also a trade item with other tribes and with the Europeans when they came into the area. There are spiritual and cultural stories that go with it.

In 1846, about half the Miami were taken to Kansas. In 1867, that land got too valuable and they were removed again, this time to Oklahoma. Some of the white corn was taken along on that journey and there were gardens that went on in Kansas and Oklahoma. But, for a time, it was not planted.

Then, in the late 1980s, I believe, there was a Miami lady who had an ear of that corn sitting on her mantle. She said, "It's time to give it up." She was an elder and she knew it was a very wise thing. Now there are many families who plant it in their gardens. There are even tribal efforts to do it as a community.

The fall is a good time of year to get the cattail root because all that good sunshine is stored down there in that root. You can hose it off and throw it in the fire. When all those little rootlets have burned off on the outside, they're done. You can take your spoon and scoop it out. It's that good! I like to soak it in water and put it on the grill. Then you can peel those leaves back and add a little butter and salt.

Jerusalem artichoke is a traditional plant. The roots are wonderful. It's a wild sunflower, so it has that beautiful yellow head. But it's very small, so you don't use the seeds. The root tastes, when it's raw, like a water chestnut. It's really good, kind of crunchy and full of liquid. If you bake it, it's more like a potato.

I believe you have to have a relationship with a plant. Approaching a plant, I think you have to understand it is an entity; it's not just sitting there, waiting for you to come and take it. You're not a shepherd. It's one-on-one, a relationship you have to put in place before you can take that plant.

You know what my aunt says to me? This food we eat is from the dust of the bones of our grandfathers. That dust feeds the food that feeds us. And so we're all connected through time, through that place and through that food. I mean, it all comes together when you think of it that way.

DORIS ARTIS WALTERS

WEAVER SETTLEMENT DESCENDANT

{ Marion }

African-American settlements are a great, underreported part of Indiana's farming history. These settlements were founded by free African-American families from the 1830s through about 1870. Doris Artis Walters is one of the oldest surviving members of the Weaver family. The Weavers were among the founders of a settlement bearing their name in Grant County. The settlements all but disappeared in Indiana by the 1920s. Today, their legacy is kept alive through annual reunions that reconnect families with their rural roots.

We met Walters and her nephew, Tony Artis, at her home in Fort Wayne. As Artis told us: "It's great knowing you're part of this history, that my family was part of how Indiana came about."

The girls would come home at harvest time

Weaver was the settlement named for my grandmother's people. I have my grandmother and grandfather's marriage license. They got married there in Marion back in the 1800s, and I guess they started having kids right away.

He built their home. I can remember the first time going there. It was really something to me. There was one bedroom upstairs, and it was bigger than my house. There were six full-size beds in that room.

The farm was about thirty miles away, so we were there once a week. I was afraid of everything—cows, pigs, everything! I stayed on the back porch. It was a great big back porch, and Grandma set there in her rocking chair, and I stayed out there with her.

But I can remember the house. There was a fence all around it. Out the back door was the bathroom, the outhouse—that's what we called it. And then through a gate you went and there was this great big garden. Us kids would sneak out there and get tomatoes. Then you'd pour salt in your hand, you know.

The orchard was beyond the end of that fence. They had every kind of fruit you can think of because Grandpa had gotten seed from some of his brothers that came from North Carolina. They had a grape arbor. You can't imagine the fruit we learned to eat.

"They would be in the kitchen, cooking and carrying on ... It was just a place of love."

All the girls would come home at harvest time. They canned all the fruit. They wrapped green tomatoes in newspapers, wrapped pears, everything. They had a cellar under the house, and they stored it down there—potatoes and onions. And right off the back porch was the smokehouse. It had shutters on it. That's where Grandpa hung his meat.

Every cow was named. 'Course I didn't fool around the cows. They put them in a thing that closed around their neck. And they had chains they put on the back of their legs and put their tail in it.

Grandpa said, "You have to learn to milk a cow." I went and I touched that tit. Man! She was trying to kick 'cause I was squeezing too hard. I took off. I never tried to milk a cow after that.

My grandmother had long braids and they were white. Her hair had turned white. She would say her head was hot. My cousin Eleanor and I were out to the farm together and grandmother would say, "Get the brush. Pump the water on the brush and brush my hair with cool water." Eleanor would be on one side and I would be on the other and we would see who could braid the prettiest.

We had to pump the water and bring it in. They had a stove that had a reservoir on the side. You filled that with water, and when they built the fire it heated the water, so you had hot water all the time for dishes and bathing. The boys kept the woodpile filled. They had to chop wood. We would watch them, but we weren't allowed to use axes or anything like that.

Grandma would sit in the kitchen and tell the girls what she wanted. They would have fried chicken for breakfast sometimes 'cause they had plenty of chickens. And they would fry potatoes in the oven. We always had rice with sugar in it at breakfast time. She'd have a humongous breakfast because most of the kids would come home. She would say, "Now you knead that dough just a little more for those biscuits." They made biscuits and corn-bread; they had a thing that would grind the corn. Grandma, she could tell by sitting there in the kitchen watching if they didn't knead that dough enough. I thought, "'Need' it? Why do they need it?" I didn't know any better!

Grandma wore a big apron. She had, as she called them, biddies, baby chickens. They would be in this apron, and she had a box behind that stove in the kitchen. She was so careful with them. She'd put them in that box. "Why you bringing these birds in the house?"

"It's too damp for them. I want them dried out."

They stayed in that box behind the stove, and they stayed warm. She didn't let dogs or cats in the house. But the chickens came in.

Everybody went to Grandma or Grandpa and got a hug. Grandpa might pinch you, but you got a hug. And the girls, mama and her sisters, they'd get together—and even some of the sister-in-laws. They would be in the kitchen, cooking and carrying on. When everybody was there, you didn't hear arguing or disagreeing. It was just a place of love.

CHRIS VOSTERS

WIBS STONE GROUND GRAIN

Chris Vosters's farmhouse stands beside a grove of trees along a narrow, gently winding road outside Odon. Chris isn't ashamed to let you know how she feels: She's tired from the stresses of having to shoulder Wibs Stone Ground Grain, a family business, after the recent passing of her husband. When we meet around her kitchen table, her main concern revolves around making sure her son and daughter are able to finish college. She survived cancer, an experience that has reinforced her belief in the importance of natural foods, including the delicious kettle corn that's become her stock-in-trade. "People are getting smarter," she says. "They've figured out that all these preservatives, all this non-natural stuff is not what you really need."

{ *Odon* }

Finding heaven in-between

My dad bought this farm in 1958, when I was born. We had cows and pigs and raised soybeans, wheat, clover. Then my dad had open-heart surgery, and they told him, basically, never darken the door at McDonald's. Go back to nature. Stay away from refined foods.

That's how the gristmill evolved. It was for family use.

My dad developed lymphoma and passed away in '02. My brother-in-law, who was

helping him, had a brain aneurysm. He's no longer able to help. My husband helped him. This past year my husband passed away. So it's just me now. I don't know where we're going from here. I planted corn this year; it's standing in the field over there as we speak.

The kettle-corn business was got into by a dare. A friend of ours had a kettle operation, and they came to this antique show that father helped start twenty-five years

ago. They came as a favor to him to help build the show, and the man was interested in selling us a kettle. My dad said, "Well, I'll make one."

So one thing led to two, and he made one. He never intended to get in the business. But we found that going more specialized and going back to nature was better than traditional farming. Now I currently lease most of the farmland and just do the kettle corn.

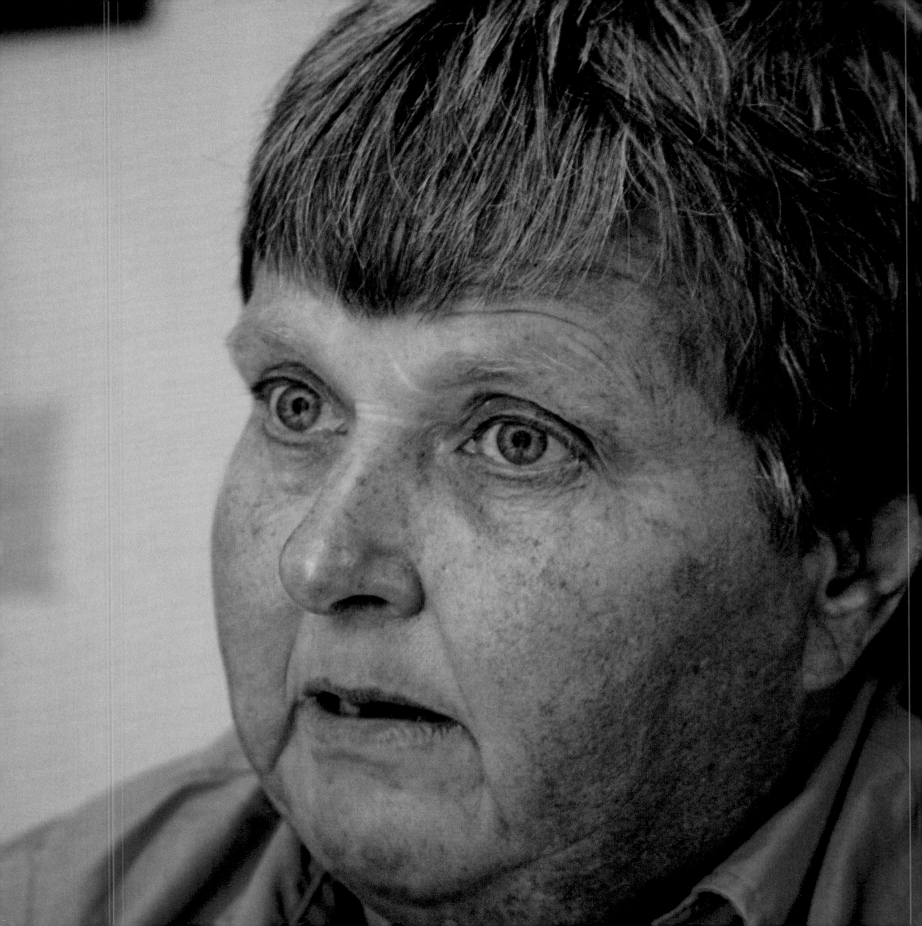

"So it's just me now. I don't know where we're going from here."

It's all-natural. There're no chemical preservatives in it. It's made with soybean oil, popcorn, sugar, and salt. And it's not overly sweet, yet it's just enough to keep you interested.

My family made kettle corn back when we would butcher a pig. The big old kettles that we used to heat the water—after we would get done rendering the lard, we'd pop popcorn. We knew a little bit about it, but we didn't know all about the timing, so ours was more of a burnt caramel mess than kettle corn is now. But the sweet tasted good after you'd ate so much grease and salt all day at the pig killing.

With our kettle rig, we've been playing the Bloomington Farmers' Market. It's close to home. It's the biggest one in the state of Indiana. It's more of a family atmosphere; it's fun. People come, they linger, they shop. They say the average food in this country travels 2,000 miles before it gets to your table. People at the market are willing to pay the difference to know, hey, this came local. It's fresh.

Farming's not easy. Back in the fifties when my dad owned the farm, we were the big farmer. Me and him and Mom farmed a thousand acres with a 4000 Ford tractor. Now it's not that way. Parts are expensive. It's unbelievable, the cost of machinery. And the machinery we've got is running on nineteenth-century time.

It's vintage! You're constantly repairing. If you can't do the repair yourself, it's just done.

When I grew up, we dairied also. We milked thirty head of milk cows morning and night, before and after school. You know, it's real labor intense. Back then you could make a decent living on this farm, but now it's not there.

I talked to the neighbor man (he farms around 5,000 acres), and his response to me, he said, "Well, you may be doing the right thing because I don't know which property I'm renting makes me money and which is losing me money." He's so big he doesn't know. And he's so wrapped up I think his grandchildren may be paying the debt. You're talking half a million dollars to a million for a combine? Come on!

Right now, corn's seven-something. That's the highest price I've seen in my lifetime. But here, a few years ago, it was around three dollars. Do you realize that was the same price as it was in the Great Depression?

Each day's numbered. It's not the house you live in. It's not the car you drive. It's finding heaven in-between. That's basically my story. I'm probably going to stay with the kettle corn and gristmill. But it's a boatload of work for a family put on one individual.

THE SISTERS OF ST. BENEDICT

SIMPLY DIVINE BAKERY

{ *Ferdinand* }

The Sisters of St. Benedict monastery was founded in the rolling hills of Dubois County in 1867. The religious community practices a 1,500-year-old monastic tradition of the Rule of St. Benedict, a spiritual path for finding God in daily life. The sisters are renowned bakers; their Simply Divine Bakery has earned the Indiana Artisan designation for five types of handcrafted cookies: Springerles, a traditional anise-flavored German Christmas cookie; Almerles, an almond-flavored variation; Hildegards, based on a twelfth-century saint's recipe designed to slow aging and create a cheerful countenance; Buttermint, made from peppermint leaves from the monastery garden; and Chocolate Buttermint. As Sister Jean Marie Ballard, the monastery's lead baker, jokes, "You can do a lot of praying when you make Springerle cookies because it's a time-consuming process." Four of the sisters, including the monastery's prioress, Sister Kristine Anne Harpenau, invited us to lunch.

The shared meal

Sister Kristine Anne: The Rule of Benedict is a short little book, but within it he has several different chapters devoted to food, the preparation of food, the servers of the food, and the sharing of the food at the table. Benedict connects the chapel, and our prayer in the chapel, with the sacredness of sharing a meal. So really, for most of our meals, we are coming directly from chapel into the dining room, here on the hill.

For Benedict, sharing around a table and the sharing of food is connected with the sacrament of the Eucharist. He ties all that together. For us, as Benedictine women, it's tied in to the sacred as well as our community life together.

Sister Jean Marie: To synthesize all that: If you don't pray, you don't eat! I think food preparation and serving a meal is a service that we do for each other. It's a

way to show people that we care for them in our attentiveness to food preparation.

Sister Kristine Anne: So much happens around the sharing of food. Three times a day, we gather in the dining room. Mornings are usually silent, but it provides us the opportunity to connect about our day, about what's happening in the world, about a variety of things, most of which are pretty mundane, but it builds

*"I think it is very countercultural in this day and age
to gather that many times a day."*

that family spirit. The shared meal really is an endangered species. We have to be very deliberate about continuing to choose it. That is what it is: It's really a choice.

Sister Eileen: I think as monastics, we subscribe so very much to keeping that as part of our schedule, which, I think, is something we need to do. In some ways, I think it is very countercultural in this day and age to gather that many times a day.

Sister Mary Dominic: It's part of our monastic rhythm. I've been in the community for sixty-one or sixty-two years, and I've had three meals a day practically that whole time. And I've gone to prayer three times a day. It lends a rhythm to your life that is so rich that whatever happens in between becomes minor compared to the importance of our getting together for prayer and people. It's presence. Every person's presence is of utmost importance, particularly at prayer and at table.

Sister Eileen: I think one of the other things with the sharing is that those of us who are able take turns doing the dishes, so that's

part of the meal, too. And a few of our sisters work in the kitchen. That's been a long-standing tradition. Then, for some special feasts—Sister Jean Marie gets this going—we do special baking of rolls and breads for the community, made from scratch.

Sister Jean Marie: Well, when I was a novice, which was over thirty years ago, one of my jobs was to work with the community baker. Every Friday morning, we were in the bakery and she baked bread – white bread, brown bread, rye bread, and then some kind of sweet bread for Sunday mornings. We made cinnamon rolls or pecan rolls and *kuchen*. And then, at Christmas time, after the Christmas Eve liturgy, we invite our guests into our dining room for sweet rolls and coffee and eggnog. It's always a pleasure to see someone enjoy something that you've made.

Sister Mary Dominic: As we were coming from lunch, I said to Kris, kiddingly, we've never been hungry. I cannot find any time in our history that we've been hungry. Very frugal people—that's part of our tradition; very frugal people who will not waste anything. That's a good lesson for most of us; a good lesson for me.

ELEANOR ARNOLD

ORAL HISTORIAN

The porch of Eleanor Arnold's farm house outside Rushville looks out over a valley toward a deep, green woods. The house itself is a treasure trove of mementos tracing a history of migration and settlement in this part of east-central Indiana. In a sense, these things prefigure Eleanor's work as a scholar and oral historian. She has spent a significant part of her life compiling and editing the Indiana Extension Homemakers Association oral history project, "Hoosier Homemakers Through the Years," an effort aimed at collecting the first-person accounts of Indiana farm women between the years 1890 and 1930. "The basic tenet of this project," Arnold has written, "has been to prove, both to the world and to these women themselves, that their lives have had value, dignity, and worth."

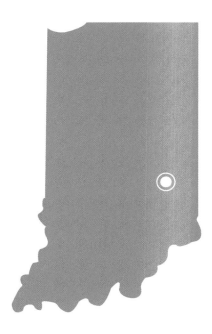

{ *Rushville* }

They really were happy

I think back how hard my mother worked, how hard physically she worked. Women weren't like we are now when we put our wash in the washing machine and turn the dial and walk away. They did it on a scrubboard.

I'm always amazed at how women talked about the good times and how they enjoyed themselves and what happened and how nice it was. One woman said, "When I was a girl at home, Mother and I got busy and did our work in the morning, and in the afternoon we'd go out and sit on the front porch and do some fancy work, and we'd just watch people go by."

"Now," she said, "I am so busy I don't have any more time to even think about going out and sitting on the front porch." What's happened?

When they had a more circumscribed life, women kept their house going, they kept their food going, they milked the cows, slopped the hogs. But when that work was done, then it was done. They didn't do a lot outside the home, and they didn't have all these demands on them to come and volunteer or get a job. Their way of life was set for them. If you did well with it, why then you were happy. And they really were happy.

Farms themselves were much smaller. Eighty acres was the norm, 200 acres was

"When I was a kid, you just didn't have bought cookies. If you had a cookie, you baked it at home. And a bought cake? Forget that!"

a big farm, which meant that houses were not so far apart. Many houses were walking distance; we had neighbors who came up every once in a while. They'd walk up and say, "Well, we just came up to sit 'til bedtime," and they'd sit and visit and then they'd leave.

I was raised in the Depression; I was born in '29. You'd think that would be the most unhappy time, but I don't have memories of unhappiness. I had teenage brothers and sisters, and they didn't have any money at all, but they'd get together at people's homes and have dancing parties, they'd call them, out in the backyard. The boys would pool their money for gasoline, and they'd get one car and go around and do things.

Schools and churches were the big centers. They both involved food, especially the church suppers, which were delicious, full of calories and one-upmanship. Many things at the church suppers were done with extenders. You might have meat loaf, which had a lot of oatmeal to extend it out. People didn't have much money, and you wanted to make a good impression.

After the Second World War, a lot of things changed. The farming changed, of course. Just about that time was when you went from horses to tractors. And as the tractors got larger, then you could afford to do more. Farmers would laugh and say, "I'm not greedy, I just want the land that lays next to me." Anytime he could get more money together, a farmer would buy more land. That's part of being a farmer.

You also began to see, slowly, women working outside the home. When women started working outside the home, they got a bum deal because they were still expected to do everything they'd been doing around the house. Now, in this age, men help much more in the house, but, for years, women had a lot more to do than they had done before. They couldn't sit on the front porch and watch the traffic go by anymore.

Women began using more things from stores. When I was a kid, you just didn't have bought cookies. If you had a cookie, you baked it at home. And a bought cake? Forget that! Women who worked started getting a lot more things from the store because they simply didn't have any time.

I love fresh things. I look at the corn that's in the groceries and I think: I used to put the hot water on the stove and then go out and pick the corn and have it within ten minutes after it was off the stalk. You just don't know how good it is. I can't garden anymore; I'm too old, but I've got tomatoes planted in a planter outside. If you can't have some vine-ripened red tomatoes at an Indiana farm, you might as well give up! I feel sorry for people who have never had the opportunity to eat that kind of food.

ELAINE JONES

THE CARRIAGE HOUSE

LaGrange County is home to one of the three largest Amish communities in the United States. The Amish are descendants of the sixteenth-century Anabaptist Christians, who challenged the reforms of Protestantism. In the late 1600s, a group led by Jakob Ammann broke away from the Swiss Mennonites and became known as the Amish. The first Amish people arrived in Pennsylvania around 1730. Today's Amish are characterized by their simplicity, emphasis on family life, self-sufficiency, and a belief in living in harmony with nature and the land. The Amish church consists of districts with twenty to forty families. Worship services take place every other Sunday in members' homes. Elaine Jones is an Amish chef at The Carriage House in Topeka, an establishment owned by her son Seth, which offers family-style dining by appointment.

{ *Topeka* }

Simple foods, simple ingredients

There's always food. If you're coming over or you have friends stop in on a Sunday afternoon, you serve something. We have food after a church service—that's a standard thing.

We basically have the same things every time, and I think that's important. It takes stress off the lady preparing it because she knows what she's going to fix. She doesn't have to top anyone else. Takes away the peer pressure.

We do vary. Sometimes we serve cheese. Sometimes we don't. Sometimes we have a cheese spread. That's a little more economical and that goes on bread just as well. If a young family is hosting church and we know they are in debt, we don't expect cheese because cheese is expensive. But cheese goes well with our homemade peanut butter and bread. Sometimes the lady would serve noodles, hot noodles. We sometimes like an egg salad or shaved ham.

But the staples are bread, peanut butter—always peanut butter—another spread of some kind and then your pickles and your pickled red beets. We vary our peanut butter spread with fruit jam, jelly, or apple butter.

Peanut butter and Amish church are almost synonymous. When you go to different communities, they vary a lot with what they serve at a gathering. But I've never heard of an Amish settlement

that doesn't serve peanut butter. We always sweeten it up, you know. We add marshmallow cream. Then, usually, most ladies add a margarine or a butter to make it more spreadable. You can go with maple syrup. You can go with honey. You can go with corn syrup. Where it started, I have no idea. It kind of ruins the healthy part of peanut butter, but it's great!

What I really enjoy pulling off is taking simple things, simple foods, simple ingredients, and making them smashing. You can do that, you know? People are surprised when they eat here. "Wow! How do you make this?" I'll tell you how. You can go home and do it. You don't need to buy all these exotic ingredients.

I don't mean to contradict myself, but I discovered champagne vinegar, just by accident. I love the stuff. This doesn't sound Amish traditional at all! But it does wonders to salads. It's hard to find, so I order it from California and I sell it. I give it away as gifts. If I can introduce something like that to other people to make it good, I don't consider that totally exotic. It's a vinegar.

I like to take vegetables and do something like a stir-fry or a salad, but my most enjoyable thing is probably potatoes. Potatoes are so basic, but you can do so many things with them. I wouldn't dream of being out of potatoes.

If you have company for breakfast, you can fix hash browns to go with your eggs and your toast. For lunch you can make potato soup. In the evening you can have baked potatoes, mashed potatoes, scalloped potatoes. You can make potato salad.

We were visiting my husband's aunt in Mississippi, and she served us gumbo-style southern cooking. When we got in the car to go home, and they asked where we wanted to stop and eat, I said, "Wherever they serve potatoes." I was so hungry for potatoes! That's crazy!

For some reason, I got to be known as a good cook. We'd have neighbors here and the guy down the road told me, "Elaine, you should do something with this good cooking. You should start serving people. This would work."

I try to be conscious about the people coming here. It's an all-you-can-eat type of thing, and I often hear, "Oh, it's just like my grandmother used to make. Oh, this tastes like so many years ago." They tend to eat more than they should, so I try not to overload them on my end.

I've cut back on the sugar a little bit. And, with pies, I use a basic, basic crust. I just go with shortening and flour and salt and water. No eggs. I don't put in vinegar. A little bit of milk? No, I don't put in milk.

To be truthful about it, when I'm cooking, I try to enjoy myself. I don't like cooking in an angry mood because I really think your personality comes through. I try to think about the people that are going to be eating this as far as wishing them well. I do that a lot, especially when I'm kneading bread. I think about who's going to be eating this and how it's going to nourish their body.

FUTURE

"These things would be science fiction to him."

JAY AKRIDGE

SAM BROWN

SECOND HELPINGS

Food can be the inspiration for many types of journeys; for Chef Sam Brown, director of Culinary Job Training at Second Helpings, an Indianapolis nonprofit that uses rescued and donated food to help feed the hungry, it saved his life. Chef Brown was homeless for a stretch, living at the Lighthouse Mission. While there, he began working in the kitchen, eventually taking responsibility for feeding as many as 400 people a night. "It's a faith-based organization," he recalls. "I can remember several times there was no food. I'd just have to go in the next room and pray. By the time I was getting off my knees, somebody was coming through the back door, and here comes food!" Since then, Chef Brown's culinary path has included training at Le Cordon Bleu culinary school in Ottawa, Canada and recognition as Chef of the Year by the local chapter of the American Culinary Federation. We met him in Second Helpings' kitchen classroom, where students were cleaning up after lunch.

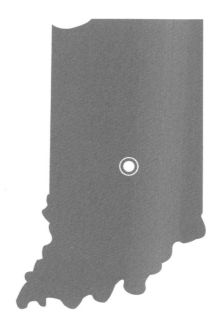

{*Indianapolis*}

I instill hope

Indiana's not a state of foie gras. We're not. There aren't a lot of people eating truffles. I was telling the students: In Indiana, every county produces either corn or soybeans or some sort of wheat—from South Bend all the way to Evansville, that's pretty consistent. It's good food, healthy food, and it's prepared very well.

There are lots of different elements to Indiana cuisine. I've been here for about eleven years and the demographics are changing. There's more influence from Latin cuisine and Asian cuisine. Some of the chefs are getting a little more into molecular gastronomy and the science part of food.

There're so many local farmers willing to share their product with chefs. A couple of months ago, the students and I hosted a meeting of the American Culinary Federation and we invited the Indiana Aquaculture Association. They sent us Indiana farm-raised perch and Indiana shrimp. It was phenomenal.

The culture is unique and, as chefs, we're trying to build that up. Here at Second Helpings, I get to see some of that because we live off donations. A lot of farmers donate food here. When pumpkins came in, we made pumpkin salsa. We had a

"My desire is to see every student we choose be successful because I believe that while we're rescuing food over on the other side, we're rescuing people over on this side."

donor a few months ago that donated a sheep and a cow and a hog—that's Indiana product at its best. It was a great opportunity for our students.

Our industry is still one of the few that will hire someone that doesn't have a high school diploma, or a GED or a degree, as long as they have basic understanding and knowledge of food, cooking techniques, food safety, and sanitation, and then, good life skills: getting to work on time, having the ability to get along with other people, understanding that you do exactly what the chef is requesting.

So our students are not only learning the hands-on culinary skills, they're also learning life skills. That's equally important. I tell people: My job here is, first and foremost, to instill hope. I instill hope and then, in the process, I teach a little culinary.

It's tough love more than anything else. My desire is to see every student we choose be successful because I believe that while we're rescuing food over on the other side, we're rescuing people over on this side.

The other thing that is very important is that we are good stewards of the resources the community gives to us. We don't charge the agencies a dime for the food. We don't get any federal funding. But we're doing 3,000 meals a day now at sixty different agencies. Many of those agencies are after-school programs, day cares, senior citizen programs. The only healthy meal some of those people are going to get that day is the meal they get delivered by our drivers and our volunteers.

My students often ask me, "Chef, what is soul food?" Well, you ought to put your soul in every plate you prepare. You don't hold anything back. I've had an opportunity to prepare meals for heads of state and dignitaries and governors and mayors. But I'm going to put the same level of effort into taking care of my brothers and sisters across the street at Horizon House. I mean, think about it: What would it be like if you were hungry and you didn't have any money and you didn't know where your next meal was going to come from? I've been on both sides and life doesn't get more devastating than that. The truest form of love is when you prepare a meal for someone who is hungry.

LISA HARRIS

ESKENAZI HEALTH

Dr. Lisa E. Harris is CEO and Medical Director of Wishard Health Services (becoming Eskenazi Health in 2014) in Indianapolis, one of the largest safety-net health systems in the country. Harris has helped the hospital become a leader in efforts to integrate nutrition and healthy foods with healing. In addition to campus and neighborhood-based programs, Wishard/Eskenazi Health sponsors the Slow Food Garden at Indianapolis's White River State Park and the city's Indy Winter Farmers Market. This work will find its ultimate expression in the creation of the Sky Farm, an urban farming operation on the roof of the new Sidney & Lois Eskenazi Hospital facility opening in December 2013.

{Indianapolis}

Other things happened along the way

We have a green space on our current campus. It's enclosed by three buildings, and five years ago we decided to take this space and cut it up into six-by-six plots and make those available to employees and anyone else who wanted to take responsibility for tending this plot of earth. We announced this at a meeting at nine o'clock in the morning and by noon we had a waiting list.

The pharmacy did an apothecary garden, so they had plants with medicinal purposes. We had an herb garden. The lab took it to the next level, and, the next thing you know, we're growing pumpkins and tomatoes and lettuce and sunflowers.

We purchased picnic tables and benches and umbrellas and, pretty soon, people were coming out and eating their lunches and taking their breaks and having meetings. I'd be here on a weekend and see our residents who are on call all weekend long and think how good it was for our patients that residents were available, but could go outside and get some fresh air.

The next thing was that we had a farmers' market. For a vendor to come and be with us, we had to make it worth their while. So our agreement was we would buy pretty much everything they didn't sell to employees and visitors to serve in the hospital cafeteria.

Now, all of a sudden, we've got really red tomatoes. We've got strawberries that are red inside as well as outside. People began to realize these things tasted good. At the hospital cafeteria, this food was served at a price that was accessible to everybody; it wasn't a different price for the good stuff.

Then other remarkable things started to happen.

Historically, it was almost as though if you couldn't fry it, you didn't serve it in

the cafeteria. Then we got what's called a rational oven, which bakes instead of fries. We did taste tests; most people couldn't tell the difference between baked and fried. Heart-healthful options became the most popular items. It was about having good food.

If food is well prepared and tastes good, people are going to choose it. We started providing vegetarian options, largely made with our locally available produce. It was fresh, it tasted good, it was flavorful. And when we started the vegetarian options every day—we tried them for a week—every day they sold out. So we made 50 percent more, and it would sell out at 50 percent more. Vegetarian options and heart-healthful options became the most popular selling items where, before, we offered fried chicken, french fries, pizza.

Other things happened along the way. We have a program where we give all of our employees a monetary incentive to achieve good health outcomes. We focus on body mass index and blood pressure. From 2009 to 2011, we had a 65 percent increase in the numbers of employees who were meeting those health goals and getting that financial incentive. There was at least a 34 percent increase in the number of employees who had lost at least 10 percent of their body weight.

The Sky Farm brings it all together. It allows us to have a deliberately managed source of produce, where we're matching it to our needs. It's also a place where patients and their families can get fresh air. It gives us this focal point where we can base educational programs, have community events, and be a source of inspiration. It's going to have a beautiful view of the city.

What all this suggests is that if you make healthful food available to individuals, and it tastes good, and it's priced reasonably, they will embrace that. And we see that even in a relatively short period of time, there's an impact on health outcomes.

I'm an internal medicine physician, so most of the time, I'm working on trying to help people adopt the behaviors that will help prevent them from getting diabetes, high blood pressure, and heart disease. It can be frustrating, and, yet, I'm a broken record and every now and then, there'll be a patient who gets it. What I'm starting to see is more patients are getting it. In the past, where I would have to think about the right point in my relationship with this patient to introduce the fact they're overweight, now patients are broaching that with me first. There's a momentum building from different sectors of the community that I think is starting to achieve critical mass.

We have community health centers throughout the inner city and we are working to create programs that not only connect patients to local farms through the CSA shares, but equip patients with the know-how to grow their own food. If you value the head of lettuce or bunch of beets you get from a farmer directly, you maybe value what you grow on your own even more. This, in a way, is returning to our roots. There's a long history of urban gardening. This used to be part of life; it's becoming a movement now.

Our larger role is to provide as much care as we can for individuals who don't have the resources to pay for that care. So we have every good reason to invest in prevention.

JAY AKRIDGE

PURDUE UNIVERSITY COLLEGE OF AGRICULTURE

Jay Akridge says he was born into agriculture. "I grew up in western Kentucky and my family owns and operates a retail farm supply business there. My granddad started the business in 1933 ... our family made its living by serving farmers through that store." Today, Akridge is dean of the College of Agriculture at Purdue University in West Lafayette. It is impossible to overstate Purdue's influence on Indiana farming. Since the university's founding, Purdue has helped to shape the state's agricultural practices and business models. It is hard to meet a Hoosier farmer who does not have a Purdue connection of some kind. The school also has a global reach: two World Food Prize winners have come from Purdue.

{ *West Lafayette* }

Who we are at Purdue

Purdue's story is very much the land-grant university story. The Morrill Act provided the foundation for places like Purdue, the University of Illinois, Iowa State. Justin Morrill was a senator from Vermont. Abraham Lincoln signed the legislation into law in 1862.

The intent of the legislation was to establish colleges open to the everyman and especially off the coasts in the heartland of the country. At that time, that meant many farmers, because most of the population in the rural areas was farmers.

We talk about three legs of a land-grant university: teaching, research, and extension. That's who we are at Purdue. And all three of those legs have had an awfully important impact on agriculture in the state. For many, many years, universities were the primary source of agricultural information. If you had a pest problem, a tillage problem, fertility problem, universities were the places you went because we really didn't have a developed agribusiness sector to provide that kind of advice and information.

Purdue started a short course, an eleven-week course, held in the wintertime. People from all over Indiana came to basically learn to farm better. This went on for decades. Many people around the state who weren't Purdue alums in the traditional sense came to a short course. Nearly all men, of course, and typically young, came to the campus for that period of time. It really touched farms around the state in a very important way.

The thing that's really interesting today is you've got a lot of types of agriculture under one umbrella. That's something that's been building over the last several years. In this state, we clearly have some very large businesses—some of the largest dairy businesses in the country, tremendous layer business, very large corn

"These things would be science fiction to him."

and soybean operations, and some large specialty crops. But we're seeing a resurgence of smaller farms producing for local markets, organic farms, and agritourism that have brought a different kind of entrepreneur into the countryside. We've got both models in this state, and they're both important.

Purdue has a lot of things going right now and is getting ready to do even more for the small, local, organic—the person who's really catering to niche markets. We've got specialists working to help backstop farmers' markets, to help them get started and be viable.

Then, of course, we've got individuals who work with the larger end as well. In some cases, that may not be directly with the larger producer because they may be getting their information from the local co-op or the seed company representative. But, in many cases, that seed company or co-op may be getting their information from us.

I don't want to forget our role in terms of training students and preparing them to move into careers across this whole spectrum. Lately, we've launched a new student farm. It's about five acres, with a passionate group of students mainly focused on the organic and local market. They've got a student club established, and that's going to give us the chance to work with that particular business model. A group of faculty is supporting them and we now have research work going on in organics at one of our farms just outside of town.

There's a growing world population; we already have people who don't have adequate nutrition. These population trends are pretty well set; we know the kind of challenges that are out there in terms of feeding nine billion people by 2050. At the same time, we have a society and a limited set of resources that have got to be respected. We know that from an environmental standpoint, we've got to pursue practices that are going to allow us to continue to produce. But you have a society that is increasingly interested in how we do things. So practices can't be done specifically for an efficiency reason alone.

I think about my granddad when I talk about plants that are tolerant of herbicides and equipment that is ten times the size it was in his day, satellite data that's helping us adjust sprayer applications based on location in the field. These things would be science fiction to him. But these technologies and others like them have reshaped the farming business. It's much larger, much more sophisticated. There's a greater investment in the knowledge of people.

But, I swear, when you talk to farmers today, you see a lot of the same passions my granddad would have seen. They tend to be individuals who absolutely love what they do. They're people who believe in taking care of the earth and their neighbors. They are passionate about their responsibility to provide food for a hungry planet.

SUSANNE WASSON

DOW AGROSCIENCES

Susanne Wasson is Global Business Leader for Range and Pasture and Industrial Vegetation Management with Dow AgroSciences, headquartered on the northwest side of Indianapolis. Dow AgroSciences has 1,800 researchers around the world working on pest management and biotechnology products in forty countries, with sales in 130 countries. Dow AgroSciences products have recently been honored with four Presidential Green Chemistry Awards from the U.S. Environmental Protection Agency, which has also awarded Dow AgroSciences two EPA Montreal Protocol Awards, for stratospheric ozone protection.

{Indianapolis}

The most exciting time ever

I was born in west Texas, where it wasn't really green and grassy, but my dad's family had been in the cattle business for decades. We moved to eastern Oklahoma, where there was a lot of green grass, when I was about ten.

We raised purebreds, Santa Gertrudis cattle, and had a cow-calf operation there. So I've always had that love of the cattle industry growing up and had it in my mind's eye that I would work in agriculture. But it was much more about the cattle and a lot less about what they were eating when I was growing up.

Since coming to work for Dow AgroSciences, I've worked in the range and pasture business. That's basically where we use herbicides to control weeds and brush and pastures to basically improve the forage and help the livestock producer to produce more milk or meat. Once I got into the selling arena for chemicals to ranchers, it really changed the perspective of seeing the green grass and what it was there for.

The job I'm in today is managing the range and pasture products around the world. So whether I'm in Australia or Brazil, or in Colombia or Mexico, the ranchers all have one thing in mind and that's how can they be more productive, because there really isn't any more land available today; what's there is there. In many cases, pastureland is being encroached on by row crops because of historically high commodity prices. Even in places like Brazil, there's a squeeze on pastureland. By law, there's no more deforestation and, at the same time, there's encroachment by corn, soybean, sugarcane crops.

We have a population that's headed toward nine billion by 2050, depending

on which number and year you look at. The ability to feed all those people is going to become more and more of a challenge. So how can we help, especially as the developing nations' populations start to add more protein—beef, as well as poultry and pork—to their diet?

We feel unique in the fact that, compared to other protein sources, these animals can be fed on a grass-fed diet, at least for part of their nutrition, which offers some shelter from the high grain prices that many other industries are dealing with today.

At Dow AgroSciences, we see this as probably the most exciting time ever to be in agriculture.

The rate of adoption and change of technology available to farmers and ranchers is exponentially different than it was in the industry twenty years ago.

Today, you bring products in and ramp them up as fast as possible because they're being replaced by the next generation of technology. From our start as a traditional agricultural chemical company, we are very heavily invested into the biotechnology and seed business. When you see the ability to add traits to seed and what that does in terms of productivity and profitability for farmers, it really changes the game.

It's important that we're located in the heart of agriculture because it helps us as a company to be in tune with what's happening out there. Being in the corn seed business, we're in the heart of the Corn Belt here in Indiana. I think that makes a big difference in terms of how we approach things. We are global, but certainly the U.S. is a huge part of our business and will continue to be in the future.

I would say that when you are able to look out your back door and see corn growing everywhere (I have corn growing behind my house), it really brings that home.

We take pride in being a U.S.-based company, but we share our technology all around the world. Most of what we start comes into the U.S. first before we go into other countries as we typically launch our products here first. So we take great pride in bringing people from all around the world to our global headquarters in Indianapolis to show them what we're doing in terms of innovation. You bring customers here from Brazil or Australia or China, and they're fascinated by what we do.

I would say, in having been with the company almost twenty-two years, the pipeline of products that we have both in the traditional ag chemical area and in the biotech area is absolutely the best it's ever been. We have real breakthrough technologies and I just hope that they get there soon enough so I get a chance to be involved with them.

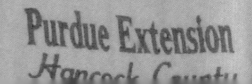

ROY BALLARD

PURDUE EXTENSION, HANCOCK COUNTY

Across the street from Roy Ballard's Greenfield office, people are working through the final preparations for the Hancock County Fair. This is one of Ballard's busiest times of the year. But then, as the county's Purdue Extension Educator for Agriculture and Natural Resources, Ballard is used to having a full schedule. The Purdue Extension service originated in the early 1900s as a way to disperse information from the land-grant universities to the public. The extension services can differ county by county. "That's a wonderful thing," says Ballard, "because you're able to be in the county, to meet people, find out what they need, and tailor your programs to adapt to their needs, which change over time."

{ *Greenfield* }

A sustainable, dependable marketplace

Here in the county, we do a lot of work with farmers who want to grow new crops, trying to find ways to do that, ways to extend the season. We do a lot of diagnostics work. It becomes a challenge because there are so many different possibilities of crops that these folks are growing. It's not just corn, soybeans, and wheat. There are dozens and dozens of kinds of crops. It's a pretty large repertoire.

One of the things we're working on now is providing farmers with a sustainable, dependable marketplace. We're pretty clear that there's a demand for good, locally grown, regionally grown product, but finding a way to get that product into traditional markets is a challenge. For individual farmers to access schools or food service or restaurants is a very big challenge.

We have a lot of interest in direct-marketed product through farmers' markets, CSAs [community supported agriculture] and things like that, but to take it to the next level, we're trying to introduce the concept of a food hub. Those are pretty popular in other places; the nearest one to us that we're aware of is in Louisville. This means creating some sort of dedicated infrastructure where there could be

"The ultimate cost of our food may not just be in dollars and cents. How the land is used—is it used in a way that's sustainable over time?"

a retail presence maybe five, six days a week; then, over time, a retail distribution/aggregation center for regional product.

Farmers' markets are wonderful, they give the farmer a place to come and sell their product directly to the customer, and some farmers enjoy the social atmosphere. But they take a lot of time from the farmer, and some farmers would rather be producing what they do at home. A hub could still allow that kind of interaction, or it could enable farmers to drop their product off and have it marketed by someone else—still source identified, still regional, but in a place where somebody else markets it for them.

If people are concerned about who grew the food, how they were treated as employees or workers, the types of products that were used on the food to produce it—if those are concerns, they need to place a value on having food produced in a way that doesn't have those kinds of products used on it.

The ultimate cost of our food may not just be in dollars and cents. How the land is used—is it used in a way that's sustainable over time? Is the water that was used on the crop from a sustainable source or is it from an extractive technology? Where will the runoff from the water that's irrigating fields go? Will it go into groundwater? What will it cost to remediate those contaminated water sources?

The easiest thing to do would be to continue shopping at the large stores and outlets and paying whatever prices [are] demanded that week. There's lots of variety and lots of color, but, in many cases, people are going against the current and saying that's not what we want. We want a smaller market, where we can go and know the people who are serving us and bringing us produce.

THOM ENGLAND

IVY TECH COMMUNITY COLLEGE

Chef Thom England's culinary career began when he was a teenager, washing dishes in the kitchen of a local country club in Warsaw, Indiana. Four years later, he was the club's executive chef. Following stops at the University of Evansville and the Culinary Institute of America in Hyde Park, New York, England returned to Indiana in 1999 to work at the Chateau Thomas Winery in Plainfield. He currently serves as culinary arts instructor for the Ivy Tech Hospitality and Culinary Arts program in Indianapolis. He is also a cofounder of Dig-IN, a nonprofit dedicated to the promotion of Indiana food and agriculture.

{Indianapolis}

Thirsty for knowledge

In 2000, I started teaching the wine class at Ivy Tech and just loved it. I loved how thirsty the students were for knowledge. Then, in 2004, I went full time at Ivy Tech because I felt like I could make a difference.

We've got over 900 students in our culinary classes this fall. When I started, we had 240. We're still placing 100 percent of our graduates. Two other culinary schools have opened up in the city, and

they're placing 100 percent of their graduates. So there was a need in the community for people to work in restaurants, to produce real food.

I also knew that if I could go in and teach more people about some of the nutritional aspects of food—how to prepare good, healthy food—that they were going to go back to their own pockets and start doing the real work that needs to be done in some of those areas.

You have this skipped generation that did not teach their kids to cook. Now those kids are learning from their grandparents or from watching the Food Network on TV. There's a whole other training that has to happen to teach those younger people how to cook.

I started going into the community and teaching people. I'd talk about sautéing and, afterwards, I'd have two or three people come up to me and say, "Okay, how

would I do this in my microwave?" They didn't have stoves because those things weren't provided in their apartments or their houses.

But then there isn't a lot of food available in some parts of Indianapolis. I know people who have to take two or three buses to get to the grocery store. How much are you going to buy at the grocery store if, to get home, you have to change buses two or three times? It's crazy. So one of the things I started doing three years ago was going into some of those communities, helping to build urban gardens and teaching more people how to grow a tomato on their balcony.

When I see people cooking with an Indiana tomato for the first time, and how that leapfrogs into their going to a farmers' market and trying to eat as much locally as they can, that's amazing. It makes a huge impact when we start to eat local and that money stays local. We know that the average small Indiana farmer will spend that money in the community. Whereas, buying something that's packaged, the money goes out of state almost immediately. It is estimated that if each individual resident purchased an average $4.50 of food directly from Indiana farmers each week, this would generate $1.5 billion of new farm income for the state.

Over the past three years, Indiana has been ranked one of the top states for the increase in the number of local foods sold. We've seen huge increases in the number of farmers' markets and farm stands; that food is getting out there. Where before we didn't see much planted other than corn, wheat, and soybeans, we've got more small acreage crops now.

Through my work with Slow Food over the years, it's been neat to see how other states are actually coming to us and asking, "How are you doing it?" We're Indiana! We're supposed to be behind the times. But people are starting to look to us as leaders. It's amazing to think the president of Slow Food wants to come out and spend a couple of weeks here to see things.

But I think there's a real divide between what I would call the slow food people and big ag. They're on the opposite ends of things and won't talk to each other. When the little urban farmer starts to realize that the big ag people are really just trying to make a living, it broadens the conversation.

ASTER BEKELE
FELEGE HIYWOT CENTER

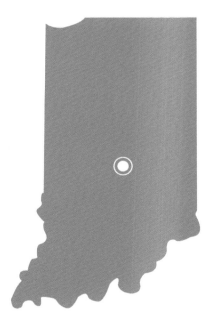

You find Aster Bekele's Felege Hiywot Center by turning down a pot-holed side street on the near north side of inner-city Indianapolis. This is a working-class neighborhood that's seen better days. An old school sits abandoned; there are vacant lots where houses once stood. But, thanks to Bekele and her cadre of young workers and volunteers, this is also the site of a thriving urban produce garden.

Bekele came to the United States from her native Ethiopia in 1973. She attended IUPUI and eventually was hired by Eli Lilly and Company to do chemical research. Bekele worked at Lilly for twenty-seven years before retiring in 2007. In the meantime, she dedicated herself to trying to improve the lives of children growing up in some of the city's toughest, crime-ridden neighborhoods.

The Felege Hiywot Center was started in Spring 2006. "When that garden started, those kids were excited," Bekele remembers. "They were saying, 'We're the ones who are poor.' But when they had the garden, it was a different story. They wanted to give. They wanted to help."

{*Indianapolis*}

The garden is a lasting thing

The children had no idea where food is coming from. They thought food comes from a grocery store. At first, they wouldn't touch the vegetables we grew. So we added them to things like pizza sauce and they started thinking, "This is good!" Initially, we just had to do it that way. But they got used to it. Now, believe it or not, we don't spray, we don't do anything, and they will actually go out, pick, and eat. It's a huge change!

We have a Lilly biochemist who came here to volunteer in 2008. He really hurts for kids who have a hard time getting food because, when he was a child, he and his parents had to go to a food pantry. He was always worried that by the time he'd get to the front of the line the food would be gone. So his thing was that the best way to help kids was teach them how to grow food. That is how they will know they're secure. They can do something.

They can really take care of themselves. It's showing these children that they can do so much wherever they are, even in an apartment, they can grow food—and a variety of food.

We had to start with food they were familiar with, lots of greens, and slowly develop that to include other vegetables. Then it became like, no matter what, I will take one bite, whatever it is. Now whatever we have, they will taste. That's progress.

FHC
Felege Hiywot Center
arden Edu
ou, as you did it to one of t
en; you did it to me." Mat

"The garden represents a kind of healing."

The garden represents a kind of healing. We have Quentin here. He's eighteen. When he first came here, the lady from the center that brought him said, "He's not going to be doing much; he doesn't speak. Can he just sit?" We thought, sure.

So he's sitting because we were already told that he doesn't do much, doesn't listen, doesn't talk. But we're doing gardening with the kids and, whenever we go outside, he comes along. All of a sudden we turn around and he's planting something. He heard us! He's listening. And we began to wonder what else he could do.

One day we were going to plant some beautiful flowers. The kids were excited and acting up. Quentin had a flower in his hand; I think he was really anxious to plant it. He said: "BE QUIET!" Everybody turned around, startled.

We started thinking: "Wait a minute. Start working with this kid." We gave him plants. He planted them. After two years we gave him a stipend. He goes through the garden, and he will weed and identify things. He caught on to a lot more. He started speaking. He reads. He totally came out of his shell. When you ask him what he likes about the garden, he says, "It's quiet."

All the kids say this is nice. They start thinking. It's life: It doesn't matter how many times they put a seed in; they see it come up. Every time they see a new one coming up, they jump, they rejoice.

They want to measure it. The excitement is amazing.

When we say, "Here's your seed, go ahead and plant it," we start seeing this ownership. "Ooh, this is mine. I want to make sure I water it. I want to make sure that I give it compost." So we started having rows, dividing them, and saying, "This is yours," whether there is just one person or five working together. It's the most healing thing. This is where they forget everything. This is where they actually can just work.

The harvest goes to all the children's families. They take some home every time they come here to work. A lot of neighborhood families just walk up. At the same time, we have a lot of customers, like at Lilly, people who are volunteering, pick some, and take it there for sale. We have been generating enough income to take care of seeds and things like that.

You know what? There used to be a time when I felt like, "Oh. My. God. This is it. There is no future generation." It was sad. It was just totally gone. But now I see the way these little ones are interested. They want to plant more. They want to stay here. They want to volunteer. And the future is much better because they know what to do. They can learn to take care of themselves, of their neighborhood. This is sustainable.

INDIANA HUMANITIES

All proceeds from this book will go toward funding humanities programs for the people of Indiana. Indiana Humanities connects people, opens minds, and enriches lives by creating and facilitating programs that encourage Hoosiers to think, read, and talk.

In early 2010, Indiana Humanities, the state's humanities council, joined Indiana's Family of Farmers to serve up Food for Thought, a celebration and examination of food and the role it plays in our culture. For two years, we invited people from across Indiana to mull over what's on their plates, how it got there, and what it means. At the same time, we challenged them to consider food's significance in our communities, nation, and world and to confront the serious issues surrounding food—issues such as hunger, nutrition, and food production and security.

Components of the Food for Thought program included a traveling exhibit that crisscrossed the state, an agriculture essay contest for students, a high-profile event with chefs and authors Anthony Bourdain and Eric Ripert, a robust partnership program, and more.

Why food? Because while food serves as a common denominator among all people, our eating habits and passions reveal the differences among us as individuals and groups. And because food provides a natural convener, bringing us together both for daily routines, once-in-a-lifetime moments, and everything in between. Food sustains us, unites us, inspires us, defines us, nurtures us, comforts us, and so much more.

Why Indiana Humanities? Because food offers us a tangible means for demonstrating what we believe the humanities bring to the people of Indiana: a greater understanding of who we are through the unique things we do, create, value, and believe.

Learn more at IndianaHumanities.org

ACKNOWLEDGMENTS

Food for Thought: An Indiana Harvest is based on interviews with over eighty people. The words you read here are entirely the words of the subjects, edited for the sake of continuity. These interviews took place in all kinds of places—at kitchen tables, in equipment sheds, pickup trucks, cafes, vineyards, and boardrooms. Needless to say, Kristin and I got a lot of mud (among other things) on our boots.

Thanks are due, first of all, to the people who took the time to meet with us. Food, whether you're raising it, preparing it or, in some way, selling it, is a labor-intensive occupation. We are grateful for the time and unwavering generosity of the people who participated in this project. In most cases, they had no idea who we were before the interviews took place; I'd like to think we parted as friends.

In conceiving this book, we set out to create a cross section, or composite portrait, of what's going on today in the wide, rich field of Indiana food. Those more musically inclined might think of what we've done as a kind of chorus. Regardless, it is important to recognize that this book is not meant to be a guide or comprehensive treatment of its subject. For every voice we've included, readers will surely think of others that could just as easily belong.

This book would not exist without the hard work of our transcribers, Karen Ciambrone and Georgia Cravey. They committed the interviews to paper, a painstaking but essential task. It is also essential to thank Jodi Belcher, Pat Keiffner, Helen O'Guinn and the wonderful team we had the privilege of working with at IBJ Publishing.

Finally, thanks to the National Endowment for the Humanities and to the board and staff of Indiana Humanities for encouraging people in Indiana to think, read, and talk about food in the first place, with Food for Thought—then for wanting to turn the insights gained through that project into a book all of us can hold in our hands and, like a good meal, share with one another.

—David Hoppe